Stack
Your
Deck

Stack Your Deck

How to Be an ACE
in Business & Life

John Thompson III

NEW DEGREE PRESS

COPYRIGHT © 2023 JOHN THOMPSON III

All rights reserved.

STACK YOUR DECK

How to Be an ACE in Business & Life

ISBN	979-8-88504-446-2	*Paperback*
	979-8-88504-488-2	*Hardcover*
	979-8-88504-469-1	*Ebook*

Attitude: .... *To my parents, who gave me the love and confidence to believe in myself.*

Connection: .... *To Toks, my brother from another, who keeps me humble, grounded, and focused.*

Empowerment: .... *To Aliese, my best friend since birth and an angel on earth.*

Strength: .... *To Shewit and my fearless girls, Soliana and Naomi. Without you, there would be no me. All my love.*

Contents

               INTRODUCTION 11
CHAPTER 1. ACES PILLARS OF SUCCESS 17

PART 1.   **ATTITUDE, ACE OF SPADES** **27**
CHAPTER 2. WORK-LIFE HARMONY. 31
CHAPTER 3. CONTROL YOUR RESPONSE 49
CHAPTER 4. POWER OF YET 67

PART 2.   **CONNECTION, ACE OF CLUBS** **81**
CHAPTER 5. CONNECTION TO SELF. 85
CHAPTER 6. CONNECTION TO OTHERS 95
CHAPTER 7. CONNECTION TO THE WORLD 107

PART 3.   **EMPOWERMENT, ACE OF HEARTS**. **117**
CHAPTER 8. CONFIDENCE TO FREEDOM. 121
CHAPTER 9. BET ON YOURSELF. 131
CHAPTER 10. PATH TO PURPOSE 143

PART 4.   **STRENGTH, ACE OF DIAMONDS** **155**
CHAPTER 11. LEVERAGE YOUR STRENGTHS 159
CHAPTER 12. THROUGH THE VALLEY 171
CHAPTER 13. TRANSFORM YOUR ENVIRONMENT. 179

PART 5.	**PLAY YOUR CARDS RIGHT**	**189**
CHAPTER 14.	LIFE AS AN ACE	193
CHAPTER 15.	GO TEAM ACES	201
	ACKNOWLEDGMENTS	207
	APPENDIX	217

*This book is dedicated to Eden Oyelola. In six years on Earth, Eden gave us a lifetime of lessons on how to live each day with a positive
Attitude, a strong
Connection, a sense of
Empowerment, and undeniable
Strength.*

Eden, you will always be our ACE.

When Your Angel Leaves

We all know you were sent from above
To teach our family the true meaning of love
Now that you're gone we have no goals in sight
We're trying so hard to get through the night
If we had one wish it would be to see your smile
For this we would walk the miracle mile
Even though you are gone you are still in our heart
When we meet again it will be the perfect start
—John Thompson III

Introduction

You can't see the label on the jelly jar when you're inside the jam.

Life is the jam. Sometimes it's sweet, sometimes it's little sticky, and oftentimes it's messy. It might even go good with some crunchy peanut butter. But yes, life is the jam. And you, my friend, are inside that jam. Through the ups and downs, the sticky and the sweet, it can be tough to know who we really are, how the world sees us, and where we belong.

This book is about learning to honor who you are. It is about aligning yourself to a set of standards I call ACES: Attitude, Connection, Empowerment, and Strength. In a world where the deck may be stacked against you, I believe we can rearrange the cards we are dealt, stack the deck in our favor, and live a more abundant life through the ACES Pillars of Success.

How many of you are so busy looking for inspiration from outside that you forget the greatness inside of you? Perhaps you study other people, looking to others for motivation, inspiration, or even permission to do what you want in life.

Maybe you are giving, serving, moving so much you don't take time to think about what, or who, is serving you.

It's no secret the world is going through a tough time right now. Between the pandemic and political unrest, it's easy to feel like you're running on empty. And you're not alone: burnout is becoming increasingly common. Job burnout was officially recognized by the World Health Organization in 2019 and is described as a syndrome resulting from chronic workplace stress (Fernstrom 2019).

The job aggregator site Indeed.com conducted a survey of 1,500 US workers to determine the level of burnout experienced by differing groups of people. In 2021, 52 percent of respondents had experienced burnout, which was a jump from 43 percent pre-pandemic (Kelly 2021). If left unchecked, burnout can lead to physical and emotional health risks including fatigue, insomnia, sadness, anger, and more.

What do we do about it?

Our culture values productivity above all else, and success is often defined by how much stuff we can accumulate. We work long hours chasing the almighty dollar, and our free time is spent scrolling through social media comparing our lives to others. Where does it end? For starters, we need to redefine what success means.

Something my grandpa said to me at an early age has since guided my life: "I can make a success of my life as I see it or as the world sees it. Success as I see it is the only worthwhile goal to pursue."

This quote has helped me navigate the highs and lows during more than twenty-five years in corporate America and led to the ACES pillars, too. I endured burned-out lows early in my career when I took a six-month leave of absence from work and spent two weeks in a psychiatric ward. I soared on the highs of leading teams who surpassed a billion dollars in sales, earning President's Club multiple times, and in 2020, launching my coaching company, Team ACES, and earning coaching certifications with Gallup, International Coaching Federation, and Center for Credentialing and Education. Knowing who you are and pursuing success on your terms is the way to a more fulfilling life.

But it was this text from a friend, Sarah, that led to the book you're reading today: "It is always great to see you," she said. "Every time you motivate and inspire me. You have a true gift. One day, we will be watching your YouTube videos."

The seed was planted in me that I could do what I thought I wanted to do: inspire others to reach their full potential. Confirmation from a good friend opened my eyes to the possibility right in front of me. What made this time different? I had received praise in the past, been onstage for speeches and keynotes, and had rallied teams and charged up individuals. Why now? What makes the difference is that now, the timing is right.

It was a warm August afternoon in Milwaukee, Wisconsin in 2018 at the end of a weeklong leadership conference I attended with Sarah and twenty other colleagues. I shared my experiences and lessons learned, and had allowed myself to be vulnerable. I challenged my own assumptions, listened to others, and came away in a much better state.

The vision board exercise sealed the deal.

It was the final session of the conference. I have always been a dreamer, but I kept my dreams inside and rarely slowed down to articulate what I wanted. Like playtime at school, twenty of my fellow colleagues and I were shoulder-to-shoulder in front of a large conference room table with magazines, articles, scissors, poster boards, glue, and the magic of our imaginations running wild.

As I filled my vision board, I wondered, "What if?" What if I could do what I wanted to do and be who I wanted to be? Who would I be? Who am I today? The pictures and ideas flowed and my vision appeared. In the center of my vision board was "bring hope to millions." To the left, two young children building what looked like a science experiment with blocks. In the bottom corner was the word ACE, the first inkling of my idea for the coaching company I would go on to launch two years later.

The session closed with a YouTube video from Robin Sharma on leadership and how anyone can be a leader regardless of their title. Willingness to take on responsibilities and serve others is what makes a leader, not a title (Sharma 2013). I took notes feverishly. I didn't know Robin, but his words resonated deeply with me and I couldn't help but notice we sort of looked alike in a bald, brown-skinned sort of way.

The conference ended and I headed to the airport, reflecting on my vision board and Robin's video. As the plane was set to depart, my phone beeped. It was that game-changing text from the Sarah. I thought about the text, the vision board, and the leader video the whole flight home. The future was absolutely in my control, and my vision and path ahead crystalized.

Five days later, on the morning of August 15, 2018, I woke up with an energy I had never experienced before. I jumped out of bed, got dressed, and headed out to the nature trail behind my house, a trail I hadn't walked or explored even once during the five years I had owned my house. From the birds singing their beautiful early morning songs to the sun peeking over the towering trees and burning the dew off the grass, I was nothing but calm. Other than the birds chirping, the world was asleep and this morning was made just for me.

My watch read 7:15 a.m. I snapped a picture of my watch, took a selfie, and made a decision. From then on, every day beyond that day would be different. I looked at the quote of the day on my phone that read, "Without inspiration the best powers of the mind remain dormant. There is a fuel in us which needs to be ignited with sparks" by Johann Gottfried von Herder (2022).

Different in what way?

Each day would be more intentional, with steps that would take me closer to my goal which aligned with the message Sarah sent me. My full potential was to inspire others to reach theirs. I formed Team ACES two years later and am now well on my way to fulfilling the dream on my vision board to "bring hope to millions." All it took was a vision, a timely text from a friend, and the faith to take consistent action to bring an idea into reality.

We all have a label on the outside of our jelly jar and by the end of this book, I hope you recognize that label says "ACE."

But what is an ACE? And why do you want to be one?

In Chapter 1, we will learn what the ACES Pillars of Success are and how to apply them in your life. In subsequent chapters, we will delve into each pillar through personal stories, interviews, and research to help you fully understand how these principles can be life changing to you. You will learn from other ACES across a broad range of industries and careers from corporate CEOs and high-ranking military officers, to educators, entrepreneurs, engineers and musicians.

This book is for the corporate executive who is looking to get more meaning out of life. For the early career professional who wants to understand how to make a mark on the world. For those looking to make a career change, company change, or switch industries but don't know where to start. Maybe that's you. If you know there is more out there for you but you can't seem to muster up the courage or discipline to consistently go after what you want, this book can guide you.

Through an easy to understand framework, exercises, and action steps, this book will teach you how to be an ACE in business and life.

Are you ready to stack your deck? Let's go!

CHAPTER 1

ACES Pillars of Success

My first day of kindergarten, my mom stood at the bottom of our driveway, anxiously awaiting the bus so she could hear all about my first day of school. We lived on a quiet street deep in the country, and the only sound you could hear was the school bus approaching and the voices of energetic kids yelling through the windows. As I stepped off the bus, lunchbox in hand, to the outstretched arms of my mom, I was prepared for a warm embrace. Instead I was met with something neither of us expected. The kids were shouting out the window in unison, "Bye, little n*gger!"

It was at that moment I realized I was different.

At the young age of five, I was an "only"—the only one who looked like me—not just in my class, but in the entire elementary school. The world, or at least my world as it appeared, was stacked against me.

I grew up in a small town, Lone Pine, PA, which is thirty miles south of Pittsburgh. The population of the town was 3,650, of whom 95.3 percent were white and 0.5 percent were black (2022). These numbers indicate only eighteen black people lived in Lone Pine. However, my family feels even this is a stretch because growing up, we rarely saw another person in town that looked like us. In fact, my sister and I were the only black kids in the entire elementary school. In middle and high school, there may have been no more than five other black kids in our class of 400.

Rarely did I walk into a room and see someone who looked like me. It would have been very easy to retreat to the corner of the room, thinking I didn't belong. Rather than embrace that small mindset, I adopted the idea that I was the special one. I was different for a reason, and I was going to let my brilliance and light shine through in all that I did. Where did that strength come from? Let me explain by exploring a bit into my parents' story.

My parents went to high school together in Bethel Park, PA. My dad was "the man" in high school: a star athlete, lettered in three sports (football, basketball, and track), and well known across the school. As one of only a handful of black people in his school, everyone knew who "Jr Thompson" was. My mom, on the other hand, was a shy student who kept to herself. Her personality is perfectly described by a photo in her senior yearbook, in which the yearbook crew asked her to sit inside her locker for a funny picture: true to her introverted nature, the only parts you can see of her in the photo are her leg, stocking, and boot wedged out of the locker.

While they had a few classes together throughout their senior year, my parents actually met at a party after their graduation in 1968. Dad needed a ride home from the party and he asked Mom. Mom was a bit surprised, as they didn't know each other that well, but she agreed to give him a ride since they only lived ten minutes from each other. They had a great conversation on the way and when she dropped him off, he asked if she would like to go out the next night, to which she agreed. They turned that chance meeting into a lifetime of love.

Their relationship was not easy. Dad is black and Mom is white. Interracial relationships weren't as common in the 60s as they are today. The US Supreme Court legalized interracial marriage nationwide in the 1967 Loving v. Virginia case (2022). A year after, in 1968, analytics company Gallup found support for the practice was increasing, but still only a small minority—20 percent—approved. Support has gradually improved over the years and has now grown to 94 percent approval in 2021.

My parents knew they loved each other, so they decided to move out to the country where they could be together and wouldn't have to face the stares and comments they'd receive when going out and about in the city. As they settled into their relationship and their new country home, they decided to wait to have children. Many friends and close family members had advised them not to have children at all. "We accept you," many said, "but we don't think you should bring a child into the world who won't belong to anyone. They will be in the middle, both black and white." A member of my mom's extended family actually made the hurtful comment that "your kids will be neither fish nor fowl."

Then, after seven years together, my parents made the decision to have children. They made a commitment to each other that they would give their children all the love they needed to feel secure in who they are.

Mom and Dad gave my sister and me the confidence to know we belonged in any room. We were confident in who we were at a very early age, and that confidence came from home. It came from being loved every day and from being the center of our parents' world. Watching Dad walk with his head high no matter what room he went in gave us the confidence to do the same. Dad would always say, "People aren't born on pedestals; we put them on pedestals. Everyone puts their pants on one leg at a time." And just like that, I quickly learned how to relate to others and embrace everyone with a positive attitude. In addition, because of the lack of self-confidence Mom had in high school, she doubled down on the positive affirmations, praise, and attention my sister and I needed in order to always show up, give our best, and not get down on ourselves.

THE ORIGIN OF ACES

The origin of ACES can be traced back to that early time in my life. It was a time when I was trying to figure out who I was, how I fit in, and what was most important to me. I know these are heavy concerns for a youngster, but being thrust into an environment where you don't fit in will make you grow up quickly.

Growing up, my favorite place was my grandparents' house. They lived thirty minutes away, but even so my younger sister and I wanted to spend all the time we could with Grandma and Grandpa. On weekends, our favorite thing to do was play cards with Grandma. She was a fearless competitor and taught us many poker games such as five-card draw, night baseball, day baseball, one-eyed jack, and the man with the ax. Grandma took no mercy on us. "Bring your dimes," she would call out when we headed to her house. And she was totally fine at the end of the night winning them all!

Among the numerous lessons I would pick up from those early years playing cards with Grandma, the most important was the power of the ace. After the cards were dealt and I'd picked up my hand, I always felt special realizing I had been dealt a hand of aces. Maintaining a poker face was difficult because I knew I had an advantage. When I played an ace, chances were high I would win that hand. And for me, winning was everything. As famed UCLA Bruins Football Coach Henry Russell Sanders so eloquently stated in 1948, "Winning isn't everything; it's the only thing."

I couldn't agree more with Mr. Sanders.

Over thirty years later, those aces are still bringing meaning, and a winning edge, to my life. This time, it's in the form of ACES: Attitude, Connection, Empowerment, and Strength.

I created the ACES acronym as a lifestyle and a set of standards to guide me.

The ACES Pillars of Success have helped me stay grounded, focused, and on track toward my goals in life. I have also observed, and even coached, others who utilize these principles to bring meaning and success into their lives. You will meet some of those ACES inside the pages of this book.

Let's explore the meaning of ACES, namely Attitude, Connection, Empowerment, and Strength. I have associated each pillar with a playing card suit and one of the sections of this book:

ATTITUDE: ACE OF SPADES
The ace of spades' power can vary depending on which game you play, but there is typically no card higher. Have you ever noticed an ace of spades is decorated differently than all other aces in the deck? The ace of spades is powerful and unique, just like you.

Attitude is a small word, but it has a big impact on your life. Your attitude is within your control, and it's the key to having a growth mindset and cultivating your talents (Dweck 2016). You can control your response to the things that happen to you, and you can choose how you're going to view the world around you. If you have a positive attitude, you're more likely to see the good in people and situations. You'll be able to find opportunity in setbacks, and you'll be open to new experiences. On the other hand, if you have a negative attitude, you're more likely to see the world as a scary place full of obstacles. You'll dwell on your mistakes, and you'll miss out on all the good that's happening around you. Attitude is everything. It's up to you to choose how you're going to view the world. Own your attitude and watch your life change for the better.

CONNECTION: ACE OF CLUBS

Who is in your club? You've probably heard the saying from motivational speaker Jim Rohn that you are the average of your five closest friends. And while it's not necessarily true that your friends have a direct influence on your IQ or career success, research has shown that our social connections are incredibly important to our overall wellbeing (Rath and Harter 2010). So if you want to be happy and successful, it's important to choose your friends wisely.

In addition to your connection to others, we will explore your connection to yourself. How do you stay grounded and aligned with who you are as an individual? What are your core values? Before you can connect with others, it's important to know yourself.

Finally, we will explore your connection to the world. The universe is a big place, full of opportunity, but that's only if you give yourself permission to step outside of your comfort zone and explore. Who you are, who is in your circle, and the nature of your connection to the world can have a dramatic influence on how your life unfolds.

EMPOWERMENT: ACE OF HEARTS

Everyone's heard that you must "follow your heart." What does that even mean? To follow your heart, you have to listen to it. And that's not always easy. Our culture tells us to be logical, to think with our heads and not with our hearts. But what if our hearts know something our heads don't? What if following our hearts could lead us to a life of empowerment, passion, and purpose?

The reality is, we all have the power within us to make our dreams come true. But it takes courage to listen to our hearts and follow our dreams. It's not always easy, but it's always worth it. When we live our lives from a place of empowerment, we are free to be who we truly are. We can express our passions and pursue our purpose without apology.

One of my favorite rap songs is "Aston Martin Music" by Rick Ross. The song has an uplifting rap at the end by Drake. He talks about never throwing away his Grammy speech because he hasn't reached the pinnacle he plans to reach. He goes on to highlight that you have to "own it if you want it." As I think about the line, "own it if you want it," it's a reminder of the importance of ownership and continuously striving to follow your heart to be your best and highest self. Nobody is going to own your future but you. Nobody is going to chase your dreams but you. Nobody is going to reach your destiny but you. And it starts with getting clear on what you want and owning every aspect of your vision. The dream that is inside of you, inside your heart, needs to be the passion to fuel you along your success journey.

In this section, we'll explore how to embrace your confidence, follow your path to freedom, and ultimately place the big bet on yourself.

STRENGTH: ACE OF DIAMONDS
"It's not about how hard you hit. It's about how hard you get hit and keep moving forward." Famed Philly boxer *Rocky Balboa*, played by Sylvester Stallone, uttered these words to his son in the 2006 movie Rocky Balboa. Rocky explained

how life can get you down, but it's your willingness to keep going through the challenges that propels you toward your destiny.

In this section of the book, you will learn how to leverage your strengths to persevere in the face of adversity. We'll talk about how to take a step forward during those deep, dark times, which can make all the difference along your journey. We'll also talk about how to not only survive during those challenging times, but how to thrive by transforming your surroundings.

A family friend used to tell me that life is not all peaches and cream; you have to *make* it peaches and cream. You can have the best attitude, be connected to a solid network, and have a strong sense of empowerment, but if you don't have the will to fight through adversity, you run the risk of being held back.

Everyone has their own idea of strength. For some, it is the ability to lift heavy weights or run long distances. For others, it is the strength of character that allows them to face adversity with courage and determination. And still for others, strength is simply the willingness to keep going even when the going gets tough. Whatever your idea of strength may be, one thing is sure: it's not easy to come by. It takes years of hard work and dedication to build up, just as it takes time and pressure to turn a piece of coal into a diamond.

However, the rewards for those who persevere are well worth the effort. Strength is not only the ability to overcome external challenges, but also the power to overcome our own fear and doubt. Through strength, we discover our true potential and learn to rise above adversity. So whatever trials and challenges you may face in life, remember: you have it within you to overcome them all. Just keep reaching for the diamond inside of you and never give up on yourself.

YOUR ACES JOURNEY STARTS NOW
We'll explore the ACES Pillars of Success in the subsequent chapters and you will learn tools and techniques to embrace the pillars and chart your own path toward success. I began life that first day of kindergarten in a world where the deck was stacked against me, but these pillars helped me rise above it all, stack the deck in my favor, and ultimately become an ACE in business and life.

I want the same for you.

I'm excited to share these principles with you, along with stories and lessons from other ACES, and together we will rise. Regardless of the game you play, where you play it, or who you're playing with, when you have a hand full of ACES, you are in a position to win. Our success journey starts with Attitude. Turn to the next chapter and let's dive in!

PART 1

ATTITUDE, ACE OF SPADES

Happiness

Happiness isn't what you have
Happiness is what you are
It doesn't cost a penny
You don't have to look too far
It comes from being honest
When you look into the mirror
It comes from having faith
Living without fear
Some people think it comes from money
So they dream of being a star
Happiness isn't what you have
Happiness is what you are
—John Thompson III

I wrote this poem when my wife, Shewit, was going through breast cancer during the fall of 2007. She was diagnosed at the young age of twenty-seven, and at a time when we should have been planning our wedding, we found ourselves researching options and planning her chemo treatments.

This story has a happy ending, as Shewit made it through those treatments and walked down the aisle as a beautiful bride in June of 2008 on the beach of Hatteras Island in the Outer Banks. As the breeze whipped off the ocean and across the sand, Shewit seemed to glide down the aisle, the glow of the sun shining down upon her. I doubt the sun, waves, and sand knew all we had gone through over the previous nine months, but on that day and every day since, we have embraced a positive attitude and outlook on life.

In fact, attitude was the single biggest factor to helping us both get through this challenging time in our lives. Shewit is naturally positive; it stems from her upbringing in Ethiopia. She had moved to the US her senior year of high school and we met at the University of Pittsburgh. We had been dating for five years at the time of her diagnosis. While she was given a bi-weekly dose of powerful chemotherapy, she never stopped working her job with the US Coast Guard. Her positive attitude was contagious and allowed us to see past the challenges and focus on the road ahead. She was firmly in control of her attitude.

In this section, we will learn to adopt a positive attitude, stay balanced, and embrace a growth mindset. By the time we're through, you will have gained tools to help you channel positivity and embrace a mindset that will lead to growth and happiness.

Let's get to it!

CHAPTER 2

Work-Life Harmony

Your attitude determines your altitude.

—ZIG ZIGLAR

Attitude is everything. It's the difference between good days and bad days. It's the difference between success and failure. The attitude we bring to our work, relationships, and lives determines how we feel about ourselves and the world around us.

When our attitude is positive, we're more likely to see the good in people and situations. We're more likely to be open to new experiences and new ideas. We're more likely to be successful in our endeavors. On the other hand, when our attitude is negative, we're more likely to see the bad in people and situations. We're more likely to be closed off to new experiences and new ideas. We're more likely to fail in our endeavors (Okafor 2019).

I'm reminded of a question I get asked frequently during my workshops: "If you could go back in time twenty years, what advice would you give to your younger self?" I always appreciate this question because it takes me back to a challenging time in my life where I wish I could have provided myself with this advice:

Strive for harmony in all areas of your life, and see how it changes your attitude.

I was living in Erie, PA, two years out of college. I had just completed a two-year rotational leadership program at my job and moved into a full-time position, I was President of the African-American employee resource group at the company, and I enrolled in evening classes at Penn State toward gaining an MBA. To say I had a lot going on was an understatement.

I have always been the type of person who takes pride in being busy. It's a badge of honor for me to be involved in many initiatives, both work and personal, and to keep all the balls in the air at the same time. To my other type A personalities out there, I'm sure you can relate.

Twenty years ago, those balls I spoke of (the new job, leadership position, grad school) came crashing down in what felt like an instant. In a matter of months, I went from feeling like I was on top of the world and could take on anything to being locked down in a psychiatric ward and evaluated hourly for two weeks. I never thought my life would take such a dramatic turn, but this challenge provided a lesson about the importance of balance and the downfalls of burn-out that helped shape the rest of my life.

The World Health Organization (WHO) defines burnout as a syndrome conceptualized as resulting from chronic workplace stress that has not been successfully managed. It is characterized by three dimensions:

- feelings of energy depletion or exhaustion;
- increased mental distance from one's job, or feelings of negativism or cynicism related to one's job; and
- reduced professional efficacy. (2019)

In the fall of 2001, I started experiencing routine feelings of shortness of breath, low energy, and exhaustion. As these feelings got progressively worse, the quality of my work was naturally impacted. My colleagues noticed something was wrong with me, and more importantly, I started noticing. I wasn't feeling like myself. I am naturally energetic, upbeat, and positive but I was constantly feeling like I was out of it. I couldn't hold my focus, my mind was scrambled, and I couldn't maintain a clear thought. I didn't know what burnout was at the time but as I now read through the dimensions the WHO describes, each one of these applied to me.

I visited a doctor and, after a quick evaluation, was told I had anxiety and prescribed the antidepressant Paxil. In addition, the doctor also prescribed me a steroid inhaler to help control my asthma, which had resurfaced after being dormant since childhood. For the first time in my life, I was instructed to take daily medication. I wasn't crazy about taking the medication because I felt like the Paxil made me dreary and sleepy and the inhaler made me hyper. This combination, it turns out, is what sent me spinning out over the subsequent six months.

This experience is tough for me to write about. It's a part of my life that, up until present day, I haven't felt comfortable talking about. I thought there was something wrong with me, and in sharing with others, they would see me as less than.

I wasn't getting any better after taking Paxil and using the inhaler on a daily basis. I felt worse, in fact. I kept doing what I knew best, which was pouring myself into my work, but the shortness of breath and exhaustion were still present.

It all came to a head one Friday in November of 2001. I was in a meeting. I was having trouble breathing, which made me dizzy and disoriented. I stood up in the middle of the meeting and walked out into the lobby of the office. My friend was in the lobby and noticed I was wandering about aimlessly and decided to call for an ambulance.

My mind was racing fast from the combination of the inhaler and Paxil, so I refused to get into the ambulance. My paranoia kicked in and I didn't want to be taken away. I was very much focused on preserving my image as a strong leader and didn't want to be seen as weak. I had my friend take me home and my parents made a four-hour drive the next day to pick me up and have me evaluated by our family doctor. I decided to take a six-month leave of absence from my job so I could take time to understand what was going on and focus on getting better.

During those six months off work, I stayed with my parents in the home I grew up in. I returned to the country, to a slow life, which was the complete opposite to what I had become used to. Rather than what we had hoped would be a time of recovery, I continued to experience psychotic episodes. I was not thinking straight, felt extreme paranoia, and wasn't at all like my normal self. There were days when I would sleep all day and other days I wouldn't sleep at all. I would stay up writing poetry or notes about businesses I wanted to create or just getting up and walking out of the house in the middle of the night. In fact, this "midnight walk" became so common that my parents needed to hide my shoes. I would wake up at two in the morning and go out, which wasn't safe as my parents live on a dark country road with no streetlights.

This strange behavior led my parents to do what they have since described as the toughest decision of their life: take me to be evaluated in a mental hospital. I remember being incredibly frustrated at the hospital. The doctors had to take away my contacts and glasses because I was not allowed to have anything sharp, like the stems of my glasses, or any chemicals, like my contact solution. I was checked into a strange place and couldn't even see beyond a few feet in front of me.

Each day, the doctors would ask me a series of questions and give my mother a report. The doctors told my mom they were amazed at how smart and articulate I was; it was those comments that made her realize there wasn't anything wrong with me. She became relieved once the person they were describing was still the person she knew all along.

After two weeks of doctors not being able to find anything wrong with me, I was taken to another specialist in Pittsburgh who finally understood the problem. The psychotic episodes I was experiencing, my shortness of breath, paranoia, and becoming out of touch with reality, were caused by an adverse reaction between the antidepressant and my steroid inhaler. The doctor slowly took me off the antidepressant and then the inhaler.

After the six months was over, I went back to work and re-enrolled in graduate school without the burden of medication.

I learned that work-life harmony is everything.

The key is to find a balance. Be open to new experiences and ideas but realistic about challenges. Be hopeful for the future but mindful of the present. Be willing to confront your emotions, but know when to let go of negativity.

Maintaining balance in your life is important. When you're out of balance and emotionally distressed, you're more likely to be irritable, short-tempered, and negative (Kandola 2020). It's hard to be positive when you're off-kilter. Being in balance, on the other hand, helps you to be calmer and happier. You're able to see the good in situations and people, and you're able to find joy more easily. Not only that but being in balance physically can help improve your mental state (2020). When your body is in alignment, it's easier for your mind to be at ease. If you want to improve your attitude, start by finding balance in your life.

LEARN FROM AN ACE: BRANDON BOWERS
Balance resonated strongly with one of the ACES I interviewed for this book. Brandon Bowers is an executive sales leader with Amazon and has worked a corporate career

spanning close to twenty years across numerous Fortune 100 companies. Brandon seems to have it all figured out, but it has taken intentional action for him to get here. Our interview took place in the evening after he put his kids to bed. He settled down in his office with his lights dimmed and a cup of hot tea. After a long day in his office and evening activities with his kids, I could tell he needed to get to a quiet place, literally and figuratively, so he could give the interview his full attention.

Each January, Brandon selects one word of focus for the year. Rather than a New Year's Resolution, this one word serves as his north star to keep him on track and focused throughout the year. In 2021, Brandon selected the word "balance."

"I look at balance as a triangle with three vertices: Physical, Mental, and Spiritual," Brandon explained. Physical meant taking care of yourself, fueling with the right foods, and not consuming too many substances, such as alcohol. He also mentioned the importance of adequate sleep and exercise.

Mental, Brandon explained, is similar to physical fitness but for the mind. Yoga is an activity Brandon has been doing for five years which helped bring balance into his life. He told me about the natural physical benefits of yoga, but also mentioned that he does it largely for the mental benefit; it's the oldest form of meditation and is proven to have a positive impact on the mind and body (Meade 2019). Natalie Nevins, DO, a board-certified osteopathic family physician and certified Kundalini Yoga instructor in Hollywood, California backs up Brandon's experience, explaining, "The purpose of yoga is to build strength, awareness, and harmony in both the mind and body" (2020).

Brandon went on to explain the third group, Spiritual: "Regardless of whatever higher power you believe in, [understand] your existence is not [...] an accident. Your existence is intentional, so you should value every day you get up in the morning[...]." Through achieving balance across these three vertices, Brandon is able to show up for himself, his family, his friends, and his career.

ACHIEVING WORK-LIFE HARMONY
When I was briefly hospitalized for severe burnout, I thought frequently about my work-life balance. However, I have now come to recognize work-life *harmony* is what is most important. Balance implies two sides working on opposite ends: when one is down, the other is up. *Stack Your Deck* asserts that the two sides of your life can work together in harmony. In our hybrid-work environment of today, there is no longer a work side and a life side when both sides are merged into one, and we must adapt our approach to keep up.

How do you work toward work-life harmony? I recommend following the approach Gallup outlines in their book, *Wellbeing: The Five Essential Elements* (Harter and Rath 2010). Gallup studied people in more than 150 countries—98 percent of the world's population—to reveal five universal, interconnected elements that shape our lives: career wellbeing, social wellbeing, financial wellbeing, physical wellbeing, and community wellbeing.

I'd like to introduce you to a tool that will help you to ensure a life with more harmony. You can do this exercise before *and* after reading this chapter for a more complete assessment. Go to www.StackYourDeckBook.com/resources to download a Wheel of Life worksheet to begin.

For those unable to access the website now, please take out a separate piece of paper and draw each of the elements I listed before as a point on a radar graph. A radar graph looks like a wheel with spokes. Each spoke stands for one of the five elements. Along each spoke is a scale of zero to ten, with the center being zero and the edges of the circle being ten.

As you rate your current level of wellbeing on each spoke and connect all the dots, you'll be able to see exactly which elements are lacking in your life. Is your wheel smooth or is it lumpy? It would be lumpy if you had, say, a five in career, seven in social, five in financial, nine in physical, and eight in community. This would tell you that career and financial need some attention. The idea isn't to go from a five to an eight overnight; consider instead what it would take to go from a five to a six?

Let's explore each one of these elements and identify how you can create harmony.

CAREER

Do you love what you do every day? According to Gallup, only 20 percent of employees strongly agree with the statement that they like what they do every day (Harter and Clifton 2021, 37). Gallup points out that individuals who are thriving in their career are twice as likely to be thriving in their lives overall (Harter and Clifton 2021, 41). If you are doing well in your career, chances are you also are doing well financially, have a good social circle (which perhaps includes your work colleagues), are in a good physical condition, and are active in the community.

When it comes to career wellbeing, there are three main areas to focus on: attitude, skills, and knowledge. First, it's important to have a positive attitude towards your work. This means being resilient in the face of setbacks and seeing challenges as opportunities for growth. Second, it's important to continuously develop your skills and knowledge. This can be done through formal education and training programs, but also through informal learning opportunities like networking and mentorship. Finally, it's important to stay up to date with industry trends. This will help you identify new opportunities for growth and development in your field. By focusing on these three areas, you can improve your career wellbeing and set yourself up for success.

As I reflect on my experience twenty years ago, I see that I had over-extended myself in my career element and was not properly aligned in any of the others. My sole focus was work, advancing my skills, and ultimately positioning myself to climb the corporate ladder. While that is an admirable and worthwhile goal to pursue, it is important that one goal not come at the expense of the other elements. None of us possess superpowers that make us immune to the needs of our body and our minds, and the other four elements help bring these underlying needs to the surface.

SOCIAL

Do you have close friends who bring joy to your life? One in four individuals agree their friends and family give them positive energy everyday (Harter and Clifton 2021, 45). Social wellbeing took a big hit during the pandemic as we were forced out of offices, where connections and friendships are actively cultivated. In the absence of in-person connection, it's important we make time to form those social connections. Research shows loneliness is on the rise, and lack of human connection can be more harmful to your health than obesity, smoking, and high blood pressure (House, Landis, and Umberson 1988, 540–545).

It's no secret we are busier now than we have ever been. Our social connections suffer as we are constantly on the move, shuffling from meeting to meeting and from school to activities. With the technology we have at our fingertips, we are a more connected society, but it's this very technology that can ultimately lead us to a feeling of isolation which has a detrimental effect on our overall health. A 2017 study of young adults ages eighteen to thirty-two found individuals with higher social media usage are more than three times as likely to feel socially isolated compared with those who use social media less frequently (Prev 2017).

Many factors contribute to social wellbeing. However, three good areas to focus on are attitude, communication, and relationships. Attitude is crucial because it determines how we approach and interact with others. If we have a positive attitude, we are more likely to be open and receptive to new people and experiences. Communication is also vital for social wellbeing. It allows us to connect with others, exchange ideas, and resolve conflicts. Communication can mean giving someone a call or meeting with them in person. Lastly, relationships are central to social wellbeing. They provide us with support, love, and companionship. When we improve our attitude, communication, and relationships, we can encourage social wellbeing in ourselves and in those around us.

FINANCIAL

Do you manage your money well and do you feel you have enough money to take care of yourself and your daily obligations? Only one in four Americans reported having no money worries in the last week (Harter and Clifton 2021, 55). With 75 percent of Americans experiencing weekly money struggles, there is a good chance someone you know is in a tough position.

The good news is an increase in money, beyond a certain level, is not a strong predictor of overall happiness. A 2010 study out of Princeton University found there's a correlation between happiness and wealth, to a point of about $75,000 per year. When people make more than $75,000 a year, their happiness doesn't increase, but the lower their income is, the worse they feel (Kahneman and Deaton 2010).

One of the keys to improving your financial wellbeing is to have the right attitude. Many people believe they cannot improve their financial situation, but that is simply not true. If you are willing to work hard and make some changes in your spending habits, you can absolutely improve your financial wellbeing. The first step is to focus on your attitude.

Believe you can improve your financial situation and take action accordingly.

Another key area to focus on is your relationship with money. Do you view money as something scarce and needing to be carefully guarded? Or do you see it as a means to achieving your goals? Your relationship with money will have a big impact on your financial wellbeing. If you want to improve your financial situation, it is important to start seeing money as a tool to help you achieve your goals.

Finally, focus on your spending habits. Do you spend impulsively or do you carefully consider each purchase? Learning to control your spending is essential for improving your financial wellbeing. Start by tracking your spending for a month so you can see where your money goes. Then, identify areas where you can cut back or make different choices. For example, if you find you are eating out frequently, try cooking food at home. Not only will this have an impact on your financial wellbeing, but this could also impact your physical wellbeing if you are prioritizing healthy eating options.

PHYSICAL

How much energy do you have on a daily basis, and can you get done what you need to do? Only two in ten Americans strongly agree they have felt active and productive every day in the past week (Harter and Clifton 2021, 63). Physical wellbeing is the combination of three areas: activity, sleep, and nutrition. Let's examine each component.

ACTIVITY

Most people understand being physically active is important for overall health and wellness. However, making the time to be active can be a challenge. It's important to remember even small changes can make a big difference. Taking a brisk walk around the block or taking the stairs instead of the elevator can help to improve your physical wellbeing. And, when you focus on your activity, this will help provide the energy required to do what you need to do each day. So get up and get moving: your body will thank you.

A recent medical study shows even a small amount of physical activity of any kind boosts happiness almost immediately. In one study, people who exercised for just twenty minutes had significant improvement in their mood compared with those who did not (Clifton and Harter 2021). The good news here is it doesn't take much activity to register improvements in happiness levels.

My go-to activity is a daily nature walk which has the added benefit of some vitamin D along with the sights and sounds of nature. If I'm not on the nature trails, you can find me logging steps in my office on my walking treadmill. Every day for the past three years, dating back to September 2019, I have walked at least five miles. I enjoy the consistency and how it has formed the foundation of how I go about my day. Just like the routine of making my bed first thing in the morning, by the end of each day I know I will have walked five miles, and that makes me feel good.

SLEEP

Many people believe sleep is simply a time when our bodies are at rest. However, sleep is actually a complex and active process that plays a vital role in our physical and mental wellbeing. When we sleep, our bodies repair and regenerate cells, which helps us to stay healthy. In addition, sleep improves our moods, sharpens our focus, and boosts our energy levels (Nunez and Lamoreuxon 2020). Getting enough sleep is essential for living a happy and productive life. According to the CDC, 35 percent of Americans get less than seven hours of sleep per night, and only 4 percent get nine hours of sleep. So about four in ten are in the unhealthy sleep range (Clifton and Harter 2021). If you've ever uttered the expression "let me sleep on it" and the answer to the problem you were stuck on miraculously comes to you in the morning, that is because the brain makes connections throughout the night: it just needs the CDC-recommended seven to nine hours to make those connections (2022).

If you're struggling to get enough sleep, there are a few simple steps you can take to improve your sleep habits. First, focus on creating a relaxing bedtime routine. This could involve taking a warm bath or reading a book before bed. Second, make sure your bedroom is dark and cool, as these conditions help promote deep sleep. Finally, avoid caffeine and alcohol in the evening, as these substances can interfere with sleep. By following these simple tips, you can make sure you get the sleep you need to feel your best.

NUTRITION

Every bite or drink becomes either a net positive or net negative for your health over the years. Adults with a healthy diet live longer and have a lower risk of obesity, heart disease, type 2 diabetes, and certain cancers (2022). Eating healthy is a lifestyle and directly impacts your energy levels and ability to lead a physically active life.

Everyone has different nutritional needs, but there are some basic tenets that apply to everyone. Focus on eating a colorful diet full of whole foods—the more natural and unprocessed, the better. Make sure you're getting the vitamins, minerals, and antioxidants your body needs to function at its best. And be sure to include healthy fats, proteins, and complex carbs to give you sustained energy throughout the day. It's also important to have easy access to healthy snacks so you're not tempted by processed sugars and other unhealthy foods. If you make nutrition a priority, you'll be amazed at how much better you feel both physically and mentally. Start today and see the difference it makes in your life!

In fall of 2001, I was most out of sync physically more than anything else. On the scale of one to ten, I would easily score myself a two. I was living a busy life from morning until night. I held a fulltime job with a leadership role within my company, and after work, I headed directly to graduate school until ten in the evening. Since I wouldn't have time to stop for dinner before my night class, I would often stop at the bar after class for wings and beers. This became a nightly routine, which impacted my physical wellbeing. My mom would call me out, saying, "Johnny, you are burning the candle at both ends!"

COMMUNITY

Are you active in your community and do you like where you live? Only one in four Americans strongly agree the community or area where they live is a perfect place for them (Harter and Clifton 2021, 71). Community wellbeing can take individuals from living a good life to a great life and a sense of purpose.

Community wellbeing can show up in many forms. Perhaps you enjoy volunteering at your local school, hospital, or church, or maybe you are involved in an outreach program. The key is to involve yourself in something bigger than yourself. Gallup describes this as well-doing, which can serve to inoculate you against stress and negative emotions. A survey found nine in ten people reported an emotional boost from giving back and volunteering (Harter and Clifton 2021, 73).

There's no place like home, and everyone deserves to have a community they can be proud of. If you're looking for ways to improve your community wellbeing, there are plenty of things you can do. Getting active in the community is a great way to meet new people and make a positive impact. Volunteering with local organizations is another great way to give back to the community. And simply taking the time to get to know your neighbors can go a long way towards making your community a better place to live. By being a resource to the community, you can help to make it a better place for everyone.

TAKE CHARGE OF YOUR ATTITUDE
Think about the last time you felt really good. Maybe you were on vacation or had just finished a project at work. Chances are, you were in a state of balance. Your attitude was positive, your career and social life were in harmony, and you felt physically and financially healthy. Now think about a time when you felt off. Maybe you were stressed at work, going through a tough break-up, or saddled with low energy. When we're out of balance, it is reflected in our attitude: we feel scattered, anxious, and down. The good news is we're always in charge of our attitude, no matter what's going on around us. So if we want to be successful in life, it's essential we find ways to maintain balance. This means being intentional about our career, social, physical, financial, and community wellbeing. It takes effort, but the payoff is worth it.

STACK YOUR DECK
What advice would you give yourself ten or twenty years ago?

The best time to plant a tree was twenty years ago and the second-best time is today. What can you do with this advice today?

In the next chapter, you will be introduced to a powerful tool to help you control your attitude and drive more positive outcomes in life. You'll hear lessons from two ACES, a business CEO and an educator, on how a positive attitude has shaped their outlook, and success, in life. I'll see you in there!

CHAPTER 3

Control Your Response

"The longer I live, the more I realize the impact of attitude on life. Attitude, to me, is more important than facts. It is more important than the past, than education, than money, than circumstances, than failures, than successes, than what other people think, say, or do. It is more important than appearance, giftedness, or skill. It will make or break a company [...] a church [...] a home. The remarkable thing is we have a choice every day regarding the attitude we embrace for that day. We cannot change our past [...] we cannot change the fact that people will act in a certain way. We cannot change the inevitable. The only thing we can do is play the one string we have, and that is our attitude…

I am convinced that life is 10 percent what happens to me and 90 percent how I react to it.

And so it is with you. [...] We are in charge of our attitudes."
—CHARLES SWINDOLL

This quote hung in the cubicle of my first job after I graduated college. A friend of mine, Mike, gave me a printout of the quote and I immediately took a liking to it. Not only was I intrigued by the message, but it also wasn't very common to have printouts of quotes back then. The year was 1999 and only 4 percent of the worldwide population had access to the internet. By contrast, 69 percent of the worldwide population has access as of now (Internet World Stats 2022). So when someone handed you a printout, it wasn't something you took for granted; you appreciated the time someone took to research and print out the page for you.

The words resonated with me because I always knew the importance of a positive attitude, but I didn't realize the far-reaching extent.

As Charles Swindoll so eloquently stated, attitude can impact your home, your church, and your company, and it's "more important than your appearance, giftedness, or skill." This part really hit home as I prided myself on my appearance and I had just spent four years in college focused on improving my skills, and attitude was more important than any of that! But what resonated with me the strongest, and what I hold on to as one of my mantras is "life is 10 percent what happens and 90 percent how I react."

LEARN FROM AN ACE: MINA BROWN
I had the pleasure of interviewing Mina Brown, Founder and CEO of Positive Coach LLC and Coach Academy International, the organization where I received my coach training. We had a conversation about her early days in corporate

America and her later career success as a Master Certified Coach.

This interview was my first time seeing Mina since I had been in her class a year prior. When Mina's video popped up on my computer screen, she let out a big cheer. "Laaa!" followed by, "Johnnn!" Mina is one of the kindest and sweetest people and she immediately created a warm environment in her coach training class. She brought this same energy to the interview which set the stage for a highly engaging conversation.

I was intrigued by Mina's story and her decision to leave a thriving career in corporate America where she held roles as a CFO and CEO of a publicly traded company to pursue a career in the world of coaching. The year was 1996, just one year after the International Coaching Federation (ICF) was formed. The ICF is currently the world's largest organization of professional coaches (2022).

When I asked how Mina was able to make this significant leap from the corporate world to the coaching industry that was in its infancy, she credited her attitude.

> *Mina shared, "As I have gotten older, there are a couple things that are getting more and more black and white. And that has to do with attitude."*

Her attitude enabled her to stand up for herself early in her career, when she was working in the aviation industry where there weren't many women. Mina was not going to settle for less than what she deserved or for a position that wasn't going to challenge her. While she was grateful for her CFO experience, she knew she was capable of more and strongly advocated for the team to put her in a Profit and Loss (P&L) role. This attitude helped her push senior leaders for a P&L business leader role.

At the age of forty-five, Mina came to a crossroads and decided to walk away from corporate and pursue her passion—coaching. She was led to coaching through an assessment that pointed out her skills were more closely aligned to therapy and coaching. Ironically, although Mina had her education and career experience in finance, roles in finance were at the bottom of the career options that the assessment tool recommended for her!

Mina further shared the importance of attitude as she broke down her criteria for hiring someone, highlighting three simple questions she would ask of all candidates:

1. Do they meet the minimum requirements of the job?
2. Are they smart or teachable?
3. Do they have a positive attitude?

She commented, "There is almost nothing I can do as a leader to fix a negative attitude. I can give them more money, a bigger office, a promotion. If they bring negative attitude into their work, I can't fix it. The opposite is also true: if I hire someone with a positive attitude, there is nothing I can do to mess that up. You could work for a crappy boss—you could work for Attila the Hun—and you still could not screw it up."

Mina's positive attitude comes from her parents. Although they were raised during the Great Depression, she says they were always laughing. So, she explained, "My three sisters and I were encouraged, taught, programmed all of our lives that if you set your mind to it, you can do it. There is nothing to keep you from doing something. And hard work, no excuses, just go do it. If you decide you are going to do it, you'll find a way."

TAKE CONTROL

By mastering your attitude, you are controlling how you approach life. You are controlling the energy you give out into the world. And by generating positive energy, you are increasing the likelihood you will be able to energize others along the way. Without energy, there is no momentum. In fact, the scientific definition of momentum equals a force multiplied by acceleration (the Physics Classroom 2022). In order for a force to start accelerating, there must be a form of energy exerted upon an object. It should feel good to know the energy we speak of, that energy can be created by you, and it all starts with your attitude.

Allow me to impress upon you a new concept, described by the formula "E + R = O," or in other words, Event + Response = Outcome (Canfield 2022). This means, the outcomes in life are a combination of an event and your response to it.

According to Jack Canfield, originator of the concept, "The basic idea is that every outcome you experience in life (whether it's success or failure, wealth or poverty, wellness or illness, intimacy or estrangement, joy or frustration) is the result of how you have responded to an earlier event in your life. Likewise, if you want to change the results you get in the future, you must change how you respond to events in your life [...] starting today."

Most people spend their lives complaining about the situation they are in. They blame their parents for how they were raised, unfortunate events of their childhoods, and more. While it is easier to blame others, we must learn to take responsibility for our responses. Our response is what determines the outcome of our lives, not the event itself. We can't keep blaming others for our current situation and expecting things to change. Only we have the power to change our lives, and only we can decide what kind of life we want to live.

Any event that happens in life—good or bad—is an opportunity for growth.

Successful people know this and take advantage of every event that comes their way, no matter how difficult it may be. They change their thinking about the event, choosing to see it as an opportunity instead of a setback. They control their response, ensuring they are acting with intention instead of letting their emotions dictate their actions. And they hold themselves accountable, taking responsibility for the outcome and turning any event into an opportunity for growth.

We've all been there. Something we don't like happens and our first instinct is to react. Maybe we lash out in anger, or perhaps we retreat inward and sulk. But what if there was a better way? What if, instead of reacting, we could respond with intention?

A "reaction" is automatic and knee-jerk while a "response" is intentional. When we react, we are not thinking about the consequences of our actions; we simply act on instinct. On the other hand, when we respond, we take a moment to think about the situation and how we want to handle it. We can still react instinctually, but if we take a moment to pause and consider our options, we are more likely to choose a course of action that is in line with our goals and values.

Let's consider an example. COVID-19 is an event that seems to have come out of nowhere and changed our lives forever. In a year in which, ironically, many anticipated as a year of "20/20 vision," nobody could have predicted how the world and our lives would change. What is fully in our control, however, is how we respond to that event.

How can you start responding with intention instead of reacting automatically? The first step is to pay attention to the situations that trigger a negative reaction in you. Do you tend to react emotionally or do you react based on logic? Once you have identified your triggers, you can start to work on changing your reaction.

LEARN FROM AN ACE: TOKS OYELOLA
Toks Oyelola is an ACE who controlled his response and made the most of the COVID-19 down period. Toks owns his own IT consulting practice, and when the world shut down, his travel also came to a stop. For more than twenty years,

Toks had been accustomed to traveling to his clients and working on IT implementation projects. Lockdown allowed Toks to set new goals and build a framework that enabled him to create two thriving businesses. Toks explained, "When the world slowed down, I could let it slow me down with it or I could take time to put myself in the best position to thrive on the other side of this challenging time."

The framework Toks created is what he calls the Four Ds: Dream, Document, Desire, Discipline.

What I love about Toks' response is that he did not take time off. When his clients began to cancel in-person meetings for safety, he shifted his focus to what he could control. Not only did he fulfill his client obligations from a remote perspective, but he also created the Four Ds framework that helped him build a thriving real estate development company.

DON'T TAKE IT PERSONAL
Frederik Imbo's TEDx Talk titled "How Not to Take Things Personally" examined the two choices we have in any situation: to take things personally or to let them go (2020).

I'll begin with the choice to let things go. Learning to let things go means recognizing that other people have their own motives outside of you. After all, when we take things personally, we are operating from our ego. We are looking inward instead of thinking of the other person. It is all about us. As Imbo explains, "When a driver is tailgating and flashing his lights, he probably does it because he is in a hurry. It's not about me."

This is an area I continue to work on. Growing up in an environment where nobody looks like you—like my childhood attending an all-white school—it's easy to feel like everything is done to you. When things don't work in your favor, it can be natural to play the role of a victim.

Imbo's TEDx Talk helped me realize that not everything is done to us with malicious intent. Instead of assuming the other person's situation and taking their actions personally, assume the best of the world around you.

LEARN FROM AN ACE: SYEED ABDUL-RAHIM
Before I examine the second option presented by the TEDx Talk, namely "taking it personally," I'll pause to share a relevant story from one of my interviews.

Syeed Abdul-Rahim is a high school AP physics teacher, certified yoga instructor, and certified life coach. He dialed into our video interview from an empty classroom during his lunch break. The type of individual who can light up a room just by stepping in, Syeed came to the interview energetically. In fact, when the video call started, Syeed put on a pair of shades, stood up from his seat, and started doing a little dance, chanting "aye aye aye!" To say that he was ready is an understatement.

After we settled in, I asked Syeed about how he deals with students that look for attention by challenging him in front of the class. Syeed shared the story of a student who he had a confrontation with during the first week of school. As he explained, "The kid was showing out, acting up, being a big distraction in the class."

Syeed had approached him, got very close up in front of him, and said, "Thank you for doing that. It's the first week of school and I really appreciate you doing that."

The student stopped immediately. He looked up at Syeed, confused.

Syeed said, "I love you."

The kid responded, "Aww, man, that is gay."

Syeed said, "I'm happy. That is gay. You know why I love you? Because I'm going to show you how I earn my money. I'm going to show you why I am a professional. They have me in the classroom because I am an expert at what I do and by the end of this semester, you are going to love me."

Seven months later, and that same student now calls Syeed "Unc," short for uncle, as a sign of respect and admiration. The student shared with Syeed, "When you first came to me, I didn't know what you were talking about. I thought you were crazy." He went on to say, "I get it now. You didn't try to take over the situation."

Syeed's response was a brilliant example of diffusing the tension. By not taking the student's antics personally, he was able to think logically about how to respond, which changed the outcome. Syeed contrasted this approach with the student to how he would have handled the situation thirty years prior when he was in the Marine Corps. At that time, they believed in corporal punishment in schools. He said it would have been very natural to take the student into the closet for a direct confrontation, which could have included someone getting roughed up! Like we discussed earlier in the chapter, Syeed's response to the event changed the outcome.

In his TEDx Talk, Imbo describes a second choice in contrast to letting things go: taking things personally. Initially this sounds like a bad idea. We are conditioned to believe we should not take things personally. Easier said than done.

Sometimes no matter how hard we try, the situation we are in does feel personal and we can't help but feel attached to what is being done.

Suppose every time you speak up in a meeting, one of your colleagues cuts you off or ignores you. Perhaps they talk over you or dismiss ideas you suggest. In this instance, it is okay to take it personally. Don't beat yourself up. You have feelings and they are not being honored in that situation.

Imbo's recommendation is to give yourself grace. Grace will allow you to confront the situation. The key is to embrace vulnerability. You are going to need to honor your feelings and express the pain or challenge resulting from the action you are observing.

So what do you do in this situation when you are being dismissed by a colleague?

You will need to confront that colleague and explain the situation and its impact. This will likely be a difficult conversation, at least before you have experience advocating for yourself. I like the "XYZ method" of providing feedback or raising an issue, which sounds like this: "I observed X, which made me feel Y. To change this, we can do Z."

Consider this example. "I observe that during our staff meetings, my ideas are quickly dismissed by you. This makes me feel like my point of view isn't being valued. How can we make sure I'm being heard by the team?"

Vulnerability is the key to this approach. Dictionary.com defines vulnerability as a willingness to risk being hurt or to show emotion (2022). Recognize it is brave to give yourself grace and honor your feelings. This will help you continue to address situations head on and not allow them to fester into what I like to call a "thought attack."

Have you ever been in the middle of a thought attack? You start thinking irrationally and end up making a decision you later regret. If this sounds familiar, don't worry: you're not alone. Thought attacks are common, but there are ways to prevent them. The first step is to recognize the warning signs. If you notice your thoughts are racing or you're feeling anxious, take a step back and take a few deep breaths. Once you've calmed down, it will be easier to think clearly and make a rational decision. With a little practice, you'll be able to avoid thought attacks and make decisions you feel good about.

CHOOSE HAPPINESS

Shawn Achor is the *New York Times* bestselling author of *The Happiness Advantage* and *Big Potential*. Shawn has worked in fifty countries with nearly half the Fortune 100 and everywhere from Camp David and Harvard to Zimbabwean shantytowns and children's cancer wards in Boston.

> *Shawn tells us, "Ninety percent of our long-term happiness is predicted not by the world around us, but by how our brain processes the world around us" (2011).*

In other words, if we believe the world is out to get us, that is how we will experience it. But of course, the opposite is also true: if we choose to see the world as a generally positive, supportive place, that is how we will experience it.

That doesn't mean bad things won't happen. But it does take some of the perceived negative intent out of those things when they do. Maybe the person who just cut you off on the road is late getting to the hospital to see a sick loved one. Maybe the gate agent is just doing their job and not conspiring against you (McWilliams 2019).

In his TEDx Talk titled "The Happiness Advantage: Linking Positive Brains to Performance," Shawn provides a good lesson on how to create a "happiness advantage," which is the assertion that our brains perform significantly better when feeling positive than negative (2011). I absolutely love this TEDx Talk. Shawn opens with a hilarious story about playing with his younger sister in his room. She got hurt and he was able to talk her out of getting him in trouble by getting her to use her imagination. I don't want to give the story away, but let's just say that hearing it took me back to a childhood memory of negotiating with my sister not to tell on me for convincing her to jump off the top ropes and onto her head.

Shawn's sense of humor in his talk perfectly aligns with the happiness advantage; as I was engaged in and enjoying the story, I found myself having fun. This "happiness" then caused me to pay more attention, retain more, and fully engage in the learning.

As Shawn explains, "Your intelligence rises, your creativity rises, your energy levels rise. Every single business outcome improves. Your brain at positive is 31 percent more productive than at negative, neutral, or stressed. You are 37 percent better at sales. Doctors are 19 percent faster, more accurate at coming up with the correct diagnosis when positive instead of negative, neutral or stressed" (2011).

How can this be?

Dopamine, Shawn explains, serves two functions:

Not only does it make you happier, but it turns on all the learning centers in your brain, which allow you to adapt to the world in a different way.

What can you do to create the happiness advantage?

Shawn recommends the following exercise to train your brain to become more positive. It only takes two minutes each day for twenty-one days to rewire your brain to work more optimistically:

- Keep a gratitude journal. When you write down three new things you are grateful for each day, your brain starts to scan the world not for negative but for positive things each day. I have kept a gratitude journal for several years and can personally attest to the benefits that Shawn points out. We also have a family Gratitude Jar in our house where we drop small notes in when something happens that we want to remember and at the end of each year, we read out the moments we are grateful for.
- Exercise teaches your brain that your behavior matters. We spoke of this in the last chapter when we discussed the importance of balance.
- Meditation allows our brains to focus on the task at hand instead of the multi-tasking that has become so prevalent in today's society.
- Preform random acts of kindness. Shawn recommends writing an email each day to praise or thank someone in your social support network.

This chapter has shown us it's not the events in life but our response to the events which determine the outcome.

Attitude is everything. The small choices we make each day define us. And when it comes to happiness, we have the power to choose how we feel. No one can control our happiness but us. This gives us a major advantage because we are in control of our own destiny. We can choose to be happy no matter what life throws our way. When we're happy, we're more productive, more engaged, and more likely to achieve our goals. We own our response to life's challenges and we have the power to create our own happiness.

When we have a positive attitude, we see the good in others and ourselves. We're able to find solutions to problems instead of dwelling on the problem itself. We attract good things into our lives because we're open to them. On the other hand, when we have a negative attitude, we focus on the bad in others and ourselves. We dwell on our problems and believe they're insurmountable. We push away good things because we believe we don't deserve them.

The choice is yours: you can have a positive or negative attitude. It's up to you to choose which attitude you want to have.

Choose wisely!

Now that you have a firm grasp of the choices you have in any situation, how do you put yourself in a growth mindset? How do you align your positive attitude toward the right opportunities and ensure you pursue those opportunities when they arise? Turn the page and let's shift into growth mode!

STACK YOUR DECK
Would you like to better control your response to things happening in your life?

Is there something you recently took personally that you want to see differently?

Go to www.StackYourDeckBook.com/resources for a worksheet on how to prepare your ideal response to any event.

CHAPTER 4

Power of Yet

———

There I was, on stage with an auditorium full of students with all eyes on me during my senior year of college elections for President of National Society of Black Engineers (NSBE). With more than 600 chapters worldwide, NSBE is one of the largest student-managed organizations in the country (2022).

"I am not a leader yet," I told them, "but if you put your trust in me, we can accomplish great things together."

Sweat beading up on my forehead and my voice cracking, I attempted to hold it together with confidence as I explained my vision for the organization. I wanted to lead NSBE, but more than anything, I wanted the members to trust that we could do great things.

I don't know if it was the transparency, the vulnerability, the authenticity, or a combination of all three, but I opened myself up to the membership that evening. I also included a very powerful word we will dissect in this chapter: the word "yet."

I went on to win the election that night and was excited to get to work with the executive board in support of NSBE's mission, which was to increase the number of culturally responsible black engineers who excel academically, succeed professionally, and positively impact the community.

That school year, our NSBE chapter was on fire; we took over the campus, partnered with corporate sponsors to coordinate job fairs, hosted weekly study sessions, coordinated fashion shows, set up NSBE Jr. chapters in high schools, and the parties! Oh, the NSBE parties. The monthly parties we hosted were attended by over 500 students and helped fund all the programs we offered our members.

In fact, I remember quite well sitting in a Dean's council meeting with the other student organizations, such as Engineering Student Council (ESC), Society of Women Engineer's (SWE), and others. We would report our fundraisers to the Dean of Engineering. SWE had a hoagie sale that raised $85, ESC sold raffle tickets that raised $125, and I reported that NSBE hosted a party where we rented out the David Lawrence Convention Center, were sponsored by the local Pittsburgh radio station, and generated $6,000.

At the end of the school year, our NSBE chapter went on to receive the National Medium Size Chapter of the Year Award and I was recognized as the Pitt Student Leader of the Year and received the Engineering Leadership Award. My goal at the beginning of the year was to give our NSBE chapter a stronger presence on campus. Not only did we succeed but we put our Pitt chapter on the NSBE national landscape.

More than that, as I predicted during my election speech, this experience would thrust me into a position to refine my skills. Through the chapter meetings, corporate events, and on-campus activities, I polished my leadership skills and developed excellent public speaking and presentation skills. I networked with college professors, business leaders, and fellow students with ease. How was this experience made possible?

> *Through a tiny, three-letter word that packs a big punch: "yet."*

I recognized the power of "yet." I didn't wait until I was 100 percent ready to step up into a NSBE leadership role. Rather, I embraced a "yet mindset" which allowed me to step outside of my comfort zone and challenge myself to grow.

Think about what the word "yet" implies: even though something has not happened, it is still possible. This simple word is the key to having a growth mindset and moving forward in life with a positive attitude.

Carol Dweck is a psychology professor at Stanford University and author of the book *Mindset, The New Psychology of Success*. She is best known for her work on the mindset theory of intelligence. According to this theory, people can be placed into two categories: a fixed mindset or a growth mindset. People with a fixed mindset believe their intelligence is static—they are either smart or they are not. People with a growth mindset, on the other hand, believe their intelligence can be improved upon through hard work and dedication.

Let's explore the difference between a growth and fixed mindset and learn how "yet" can play a big part in developing a winning attitude.

GROWTH VS. FIXED MINDSET

Carol Dweck defines a growth mindset as individuals who believe their talents can be developed through hard work, good strategies, and input from others (Dweck 2016). On the other end of the spectrum are those with a fixed mindset who believe their talents are innate gifts that are set in stone.

Too often, people give up when they encounter setbacks. They tell themselves they're not good enough, smart enough, or talented enough to achieve their goals. Think back to the NSBE election. It would have been easy to tell myself I wasn't ready. This fixed mindset prevents us from taking risks and trying new things. The result is a life lived in mediocrity.

Dweck explains that "in a fixed mindset, students tell us effort and difficulty make us feel dumb. But in a growth mindset, that's when their neurons are firing and growing and that's when they are getting smarter" (Dweck 2016).

When we incorporate "yet" into our mindset, we open ourselves up to new possibilities. We realize just because we haven't accomplished something yet doesn't mean we never will.

It's this attitude of hope and possibility that allows us to take risks, face challenges head-on, and ultimately achieve our biggest goals.

We will talk more about adversity later, however, there is a tie between a growth mindset and adversity.

Dweck's research has shown that people with a growth mindset are more likely to persevere in the face of setbacks and to achieve success in their chosen field. They are also more likely to embrace challenge and to view failure as an opportunity to learn and grow (2022). On the other hand, people with a fixed mindset are more likely to give up in the face of adversity and to view failure as a sign of personal inadequacy (Parker 2015).

Dweck goes on to explain, "Why waste time proving over and over how great you are, when you could be getting better? Why hide deficiencies instead of overcoming them? Why look for friends or partners who will just shore up your self-esteem instead of ones who will also challenge you to grow? And why seek out the tried and true, instead of experiences that will stretch you? The passion for stretching yourself and sticking to it, even (or especially) when it's not going well, is the hallmark of the growth mindset. This is the mindset that allows people to thrive during some of the most challenging times in their lives" (Dweck 2008).

How do you know if you have a growth or fixed mindset? In her book, Dweck shares one example: an interviewer asked people what they would do if they got a C+ on a midterm exam and then got a parking ticket. Faced with accumulated events, people with fixed mindsets said this situation would prove that "the world is out to get me" or they were "losers or idiots." People with a growth mindset said "they would work harder in school and park more carefully" (Dweck 2008).

Which would you be? Would you get down on yourself, as the fixed mindset person would do, or would you simply work harder and be more careful?

Now that you know the benefits of a growth mindset, how can you adopt this into your approach toward life? Dweck explains human beings can be taught how to reach in new ways, how to face challenges and think differently.

Athletes are a good example of this. When athletes with a growth mindset challenged themselves, they developed positive character traits and did not dwell on winning alone. They focused on the process and enjoyed the challenge. Hall of Fame Coach John Wooden felt the same way. He rarely discussed wins and losses in his pregame speech. Instead he focused on making sure his players were willing to give 100 percent and leave everything on the court (Allan 2015).

It turns out, the key to a growth mindset can be linked to quantity over quality. David Bayles and Ted Orland have collaborated on a significant number of artistic ventures over the past thirty-five years. They have co-taught masterclass workshops on a variety of topics dealing with artistic development and are co-authors of the best-selling book *Art & Fear*. In their book, they explore the relationship between quantity and quality in art through a fascinating story about a ceramics teacher:

> *The ceramics teacher announced he was dividing the class into two groups. All those on the left side of the studio, he said, would be graded*

solely on the quantity of work they produced, all those on the right solely on its quality.

His procedure was simple: on the final day of class he would bring in his bathroom scales and weigh the work of the "quantity" group: fifty pounds of pots rated an A, forty pounds a B, and so on. Those being graded on "quality," however, needed to produce only one pot—albeit a perfect one—to get an A.

Well, grading time came and a curious fact emerged: the works of highest quality were all produced by the group being graded for quantity!

It seems that while the "quantity" group was busily churning out piles of work—and learning from their mistakes—the "quality" group had sat around theorizing about perfection, and in the end had little more to show for their efforts than grandiose theories and a pile of dead clay (Bales 1993).

This story gives us the blueprint to developing a growth mindset: quantity. If you want to become a better writer, take the time to write more. If you want to become a better golfer, practice more. If you want to learn an instrument, put time in daily. You are not a failure if it does not come naturally to you. Focus on and enjoy the process and the gains and knowledge will increase over time.

EMBRACING A GROWTH MINDSET

Mike Tomlin, head coach of the Pittsburgh Steelers, is a great example of someone with a growth mindset. He's always looking for ways to improve, even after winning a Super Bowl in his second season as head coach in 2008. He doesn't shy away from tough challenges:

> *"I realized if you're going to have special outcomes, you got to be comfortable being uncomfortable" (2022).*

Imagine coming home after losing a hard-fought game in which some questionable calls had been made by the officials. Your mother is there in the kitchen, making lunch for the family and ready to embrace you with a warm hug and a grilled cheese sandwich. As you walk in, she claims, "Those were some bad calls by the refs!"

How do you respond? Do you engage and talk about how your team was treated unfairly?

Or do you own the performance and embrace the loss for what it was: an opportunity to build on what went right and correct the wrongs. If you chose the latter, you would be aligned with Coach Tomlin.

As Coach Tomlin explained on *The Pivot Podcast*, "I'm like, Ma get out of here with that. I don't need that. It stings my ears. I've trained myself to hate it, because hating it keeps me upright, keeps our program upright. […] I resist comfort. I ask my guys to resist comfort, right? Guys that played for me, they can tell you, one of my sayings, I got a lot of sayings, is […] 'Don't seek comfort.' Seeking comfort is a natural human condition, right? We all want to be comfortable."

He goes on, saying, "I've just trained myself over the years to resist comfort and so [to] appreciate my resume is seeking comfort. You know what I mean? I get my [butt] whipped and I say, 'Uh, but my resume is such and such.'"

"But I'm still a Super Bowl champ," Tomlin pointed out. "Yeah, that's seeking comfort!" (2022).

NO FEAR, NO LIMITS
Sara Blakely, once a door-to-door fax machine salesperson, launched the billion-dollar company Spanx in 2000. She founded the company in the late 1990s despite having no fashion, retail, or business leadership experience.

What was the key to Blakely's success? Leaning into fear and embracing a no-limit mindset.

Blakely's dad would often encourage her to fail. He would ask, "How did you fail today?" (2020).

He was teaching her how to redefine failure.

Going through life, Blakely often failed when she didn't try because she was scared. She would excitedly share, "I tried out for this play and I was horrible!"

Her dad would give her a high five and shout, "Way to go!" He would then take it a step further by asking, "What positive came from it?" This question served as a way to retrain her brain to focus on the positive in any situation.

Fear of failure is something that can hold us back from our highest and best self: "One doesn't discover new lands without losing sight of the shore for a very long time" (2022). If we let our fear hold us back, it would be impossible to discover new lands or stretch our limits toward our goals or dreams.

Sometimes just asking yourself "what is the best that could happen?" can make all the difference. Rather than thinking "what if I fail?" think, "what if I succeed?" What if I succeed beyond my wildest imagination?

Blakely explained, "When I was a teenager, I went through a really difficult time in my life. My parents had gotten divorced and my friend was run over and killed by a car in front of me. My dad handed me a set of tapes by Dr. Wayne Dyer called *How to Be a No-Limit Person* and I started listening to it all the time. I played it in my car on the way to school, on the way to and from parties (my friends refused to ride with me because of it), and sometimes I would just get in my car and drive for hours just to listen to it.

"Long before I started Spanx, I worked on my mindset, which wasn't being taught in school. In school, they taught us *what* to think, but Wayne Dyer taught me *how* to think. Self-education is so important to your development as a person and it's the very thing that sets you apart from everyone else" (2022).

LEARN FROM AN ACE: TOKS OYELOLA

In my interview with entrepreneur Toks Oyelola, he shared an important lesson about growth and its tie to failure. Failure, Toks explained, is a relative term. He has failed at times, but he views failure as a temporary word: "It may slow you down, it may bring you down or bring you to a halt, but that failure is also meant to give you a lesson. It gives you a gem which can be used to prepare you for something down the road. As long as you take a lesson from the failure, the universe will always give you a chance to cash that lesson in."

Toks went on to discuss some of the entrepreneurial pursuits he launched that did not turn into a success. The first venture was a business where he was looking to provide solar solutions to power-challenged countries. While the idea was good, Toks described the startup and scaling costs to be prohibitive. He also once partnered with several business associates to launch a health and wellness company that was aligned to alternative healing, but the business never really took off.

Toks explained, "You take lessons from these missteps to help prepare you for the next venture. It's this willingness to step outside of your comfort zone to learn and grow which leads you on the path toward success. I don't look at any of the business as failed businesses, I just look at those business as ones that didn't take off the way I would have wanted them to."

Toks has gone on to launch a highly successful consulting firm, real estate development company, and dog breeding business. Each one of these businesses were launched after the failure of his first two business. Toks shared, "No one asks you how many times you failed; we only remember the times you succeeded."

Success is not a straight line. It's a zigzag. It's messy, intricate, and complicated. And it definitely doesn't look like what we've been socialized to believe what it looks like.

Success is getting back up after we've been knocked down again and again and again. It's learning from our failures, making adjustments, and trying again. If we want to achieve success, we have to be okay with unsuccessful attempts. We have to accept that there will be missed shots and lost games along the way. We have to be willing to fail. Only then will we have the chance to taste success.

When we're faced with new challenges, we have the opportunity to learn and expand our capabilities. So don't be afraid to step out of your comfort zone and embrace the challenge. Remember, growth doesn't happen in your comfort zone; it happens when you've stretched outside it.

The power of "yet" is a simple but profound tool that can help shift your mindset from one of fixed thinking to one of growth. Embracing a growth mindset and stepping outside of your comfort zone is the key to unlocking your potential for further learning and achievement.

STACK YOUR DECK
Where does "yet" apply in your life? Is there something you haven't accomplished "yet" that you need to take action on? What is the first action you could take?

When was the last time you failed?

How could you embrace more of a growth mindset?

Go to www.StackYourDeckBook.com/resources for an exercise to help you develop a growth mindset.

PART 2

CONNECTION, ACE OF CLUBS

Sunshine

Footprints in the sand
Gently take my hand
On the road to anywhere
I promise to take you there
We'll walk this road together
As the wind pushes us along
Our life is full of blessings
Together we can't go wrong
Today is full of sunshine
Because I have you in my life
Tomorrow will be sunshine
Because I have you as my wife
—John Thompson III

My wife and I got married in the Outer Banks in June of 2008. Fresh from her battle with breast cancer the year before, I wrote this poem as a tribute to that journey and the road ahead.

Traditional Ethiopian weddings have over 500 attendees, but we decided to go in the opposite direction and have a small gathering of our closest twenty friends and family. We rented a ten-room mansion on Hatteras Island for the week, which culminated in our wedding ceremony at the end of the week.

It feels like it was yesterday when I was standing at the edge of the beach, waves crashing behind me as I faced the sprawling mansion on the horizon. As my wife strolled with her father from the house to the beach, her white gown flowing, she looked like an angel gliding across the sand. In that moment, I was truly connected to what was most important in life.

It's not possible for me to talk about connection without starting with the special connection I have had with my wife over the past twenty years. From our early days in college together to now, our connection has helped keep me grounded over the years and focused on what matters most. Our foundation of connection started as college friends and has been built on a mutual trust and respect for one another. Through the ups and downs of life, this connection has kept us both on track toward being our best and highest selves.

In this section, we will discuss the importance of connection and steps you can take to ensure that you are strongly connected to who you are and where you are going. We'll learn about the three areas of connection: connection to yourself, connection to others, and connection to the world. You will also hear from some ACES and learn about how they have fostered strong connections throughout life.

CHAPTER 5

Connection to Self

Connection. We all need it. We all crave it. We are, after all, social animals. We were born to connect with our mothers, with our families, with our tribe. And it's this connection that gives our lives meaning and purpose.

What does that word mean to you? Connection is defined as "the state of being connected," but what does it really mean?

When you think of connection, it's easy to only consider who are you connected to. I want to give you a different way to think about connection, and I'll give you a hint: Connection starts with you.

I have associated connection to the ace of clubs. Who is in your club? The operative word in that sentence is "your." Before you think about who you want in your club, it's important to recognize this is your club to begin with and you get to set the rules.

But what happens when we're disconnected from the things that matter to us? When we're cut off from the people we love?

It's in these moments of disconnection we often find ourselves lost and adrift, searching for something to hold on to.

According to the Cigna US Loneliness Index of 2020, three out of every five adults, or 61 percent, report they sometimes or always feel lonely. Among workers aged eighteen to twenty-two, 73 percent report sometimes or always feeling alone, a leap from 69 percent a year prior (2020).

It's in these moments of loneliness we need someone, or something, to show us the way back to connection.

For me, an example of that person is actor and author Matthew McConaughey. He's connected to himself, to his family, to his work, to the universe. And he's always chasing something, looking forward to something, and running his own race.

Three things are essential in order to succeed in anything you do in life: a connection to yourself, a connection to others, and a connection to the world around you. For McConaughey, these three things led him to pursue his passion for movies outside of romantic comedy.

McConaughey first found success in romantic comedies, but he quickly realized they weren't fulfilling his need for creative expression. He yearned to tell stories that would connect with people on a deeper level and allow him to explore a wider range of emotions. This led him to branch out into other genres, such as drama and action.

In order to truly succeed at anything, you must be willing to follow your heart and pursue your passions. McConaughey's story is a testament to this truth. By following his dreams, he has been able to create an impressive body of work that has connected with people all over the world.

McConaughey holds a prime corner location on my vision board that is hung in my office, along with a photo celebrating his Best Actor win at the 86th Oscars in 2014 for the movie Dallas Buyer's Club. His acceptance speech was one for the ages. In this three-minute speech, he outlined three things he needs each day: something to look up to, something to look forward to, and someone to chase (YouTube 2014).

Let's explore each of these principles and how they can help you stay connected to what is most important in life.

SOMETHING TO LOOK UP TO
As a religious person, McConaughey looks up to God. He acknowledged he lives a blessed life and for that he is grateful. He went on to make a bold statement:

"It is a scientific fact that gratitude reciprocates."

Upon further examination and research on this statement, I discovered the work of Robert Emmons, the world's leading scientific expert on gratitude, who pointed out that gratitude is, in fact, good for our bodies, our minds, and our relationships (Emmons 2010).

Emmons explains gratitude has two components. True gratitude affirms goodness: life is good and there are a number of good things in our lives. True gratitude also recognizes where all those good things come from. That is what McConaughey alluded to. There is a source of goodness outside of oneself. In a humble dependence, we recognize there are other forces that provided this benefit to us (2010).

SOMETHING TO LOOK FORWARD TO

McConaughey looks forward to seeing his family. His late father taught him what it means to be a man. His mother taught him how to respect himself, which then allowed him to better respect others.

Connection with our family—blood relatives or chosen family alike—is critical. We want to make our families proud. Connection with family is critical because it allows us to have a support system we can rely on and trust. As McConaughey explained, family teaches us the importance of respect both for ourselves and others. By modeling this behavior, they set the foundation for us to develop strong relationships with others built on mutual respect.

Connection with family is also important because it provides a sense of belonging. In a world that can often feel cold and lonely, it is comforting to know we have a group of people who will always love and support us no matter what. When we make mistakes, they are there to help us learn from them and grow into better people. And when we achieve something great, they are the first ones to celebrate our successes with us. Connection with family gives us a sense of identity.

We learn about who we are—both good and bad—from the people who know us best.

Recent studies back this up. Researchers surveyed over 37,000 children in twenty-six countries and found adolescents who reported having a great bond with their family also reported they were succeeding in life (Whitaker 2022).

The day he won, McConaughey's voice was trembling as he looked out into the audience to his wife Camila and called the names of his three children, sharing that "the courage and significance you give me every day I go out the door is unparalleled. You are the four people in my life who I want to make most proud of me."

SOMEONE TO CHASE
When McConaughey was fifteen years old, a friend asked him who his hero was and he said, "Give me two weeks and I'll tell you."

His friend returned two weeks later and asked, "Who is your hero?"

McConaughey replied, "My hero is me in ten years."

When he turned twenty-five, his friend asked, "Are you now your hero?"

"Not even close!"

"Why not?" she exclaimed.

McConaughey explained, "My hero is always me in ten years."

Every day, McConaughey's hero is ten years away. He knows he will never *be* his hero. He is fine with it as it gives him something to keep chasing.

I have "competition" as my number one strength according to CliftonStrengths, so I can strongly relate to McConaughey's point about wanting someone to chase. For those who aren't familiar, CliftonStrengths is a performance-based tool that helps you uncover your innate talents. CliftonStrengths includes a 177-question assessment that helps you identify and rank your talents from one to thirty-four.

While competition can be good because it keeps you sharp and always looking to give your best, there can be drawbacks. One in particular is you are always aware of the playing field and the other competitors. Rather than running your own race, it's tempting to size yourself up in comparison to others. Comparison can be not only the thief of joy, but also be the thief of progress. While you are busy comparing yourself to someone at a single moment in time, they have since surpassed you.

McConaughey's third point is a strong alternative to comparing yourself to others. Compare yourself only to you in ten years. I like two things about this idea. You in ten years is always moving, because each day is ten years away. You are also acknowledging that you are your greatest hero. You are looking inward, not outward, for someone to look up to.

The doorway to success opens inward not outward.

You recognize the potential you have, and you are acknowledging you are worth chasing. It's a heavy burden, but one worth carrying as you owe it to yourself to continue to be your best and highest self and by chasing yourself, you are continuing to light a fire under the you of today.

In an Academy of Motion Pictures Arts and Sciences segment titled "Beyond the Oscar Speech," McConaughey provided some additional context on that day and explained "someone to chase" is a form of "someone to look up to": it's just the mortal version (2021). McConaughey sees it as aligning himself to who is he going to become.

LEARN FROM AN ACE: WAYNA

I had a chance to interview Grammy-nominated musician Wayna, who shared the importance of a connection that is grounded in humility. She tuned in from her home studio, taking a break from the recording of a new album.

On the topic of connection, Wayna explained, "You can't channel something greater than yourself when you're taking credit for how great you are. […] In order to let God come through, you have to be humble. So if I want to be amazing then I know I have to be humble. Otherwise, God is like, I can't get it. So that's number one. […] Number two, you know, people help humble me. When you are honest and vulnerable, people go out of their way to help you."

Wayna further explained that it is not always easy to remain connected to yourself because we all have an ego that can get in our way. Sometimes it not easy for us to check ourselves but in those moments, she pointed out, the universe can also check us.

Wayna shared an experience where the universe, in fact, did step in and reminded her of the importance of that connection to yourself and your higher power. It was early in her career and she was new to being on stage so she studied artists she admired, like R&B artist Raheem DeVaughn. She knew she wanted to create that same magic.

As Wayna's audience began to grow, she was losing herself in those moments of magic on stage and had flashes of experiencing those highs that were typical for artists she admired. At the end of those nights, she would look back in awe and think, "Wow, we had that magic."

Each show was better than the previous night and the energy was amplified.

She then recalled a night when someone picked out an outfit for her and when she looked into the mirror, she thought "I got this!" She was feeling her outfit and feeling herself and she knew the performance was going to be top notch.

Wayna explained, "That show […] I crashed and burned! The show was the worst, just dead, no emotion, no spirit." Wayna further explained, "I learned that day, I don't care what I did yesterday, or how cute I think I look today.

If I don't humble myself, submit, and be open to whatever I am praying on, it will not allow me to reach magic level.

It might be good, but it won't reach magic level. I always want to reach magic level because that is what feels best to me."

Connection is much more than your connection to others. Connection starts with you. It's about knowing who you are and being connected to something outside of yourself. It's about being excited about the future, living for your family, and making them proud. It's also about holding yourself to a high standard and always chasing yourself, not others. It's about being humble, centered, and grounded.

Connection is not just about having someone to look up to, but it's also about having someone or something to look forward to and chase. We all need someone to look up to, whether it's a friend, family member, or even a celebrity. But at the end of the day, it's most important to stay connected to yourself.

STACK YOUR DECK
Who do you look up to?

Who do you look forward to?

Who do you chase?

CHAPTER 6

Connection to Others

My late maternal grandfather, Maurice Van Dyke, sent me an envelope every month when I was in college and early into my professional career with articles and newspaper clippings and a handwritten note of encouragement.

> *Grandpa would always close with an, "I love you" or, "I'm proud of you, buddy," and these words: "Choose your friends wisely."*

These words really didn't resonate with me much at the time because I always had good friends who were doing a lot of the things I was doing. As I reflect on that advice, I absolutely understand why these were his go-to words for me. His advice aligns closely with Jim Rohn's quote: "You're the average of the five people you spend the most time with" (2022).

In the last chapter, we talked about the importance of your internal connection to yourself. In this chapter, we will explore your external connection: your connection to others. I'll introduce you to a tool I created, the FACE framework, that will help you assess your network and create a circle of friends who can provide the right level of support and guidance to keep you on track toward your goals.

I am blessed and fortunate to have a tight circle of individuals with whom I have been close friends for over twenty years. We met in college and have been supporting one another since those early days and held onto the belief that when one of us rises, we all rise. My friends live by the Eleanor Roosevelt quote, which states, "Great minds discuss ideas. Average minds discuss events. Small minds discuss people" (2022).

Thinking about the qualities these individuals bring to me and my life, I can summarize with the acronym FACE: Focus, Accountable, Challenge, Elevate. Let's explore the components of FACE and their impact on your success journey.

FOCUS

The people in your life help you keep your eyes on the prize. Good friends are always there to offer guidance and encourage you to spend your time wisely. Through life's ups and downs, they help you see past the noise so you can focus on only what matters most: you!

Research reveals a single distraction can take you thirty minutes to get back to your mental focus (Rainone 2016). Distractions can be costly as well. A 2005 study highlighted an annual cost of $588 billion attributed to distractions in the United States alone (Basex 2005). Interruptions at work can be maddening. Researchers at the University of California, Irvine, found after careful observation that the typical office worker is interrupted or switches tasks, on average, every three minutes and five seconds. And it can take twenty-three minutes and fifteen seconds just to get back to where they left off. Jonathan Spira, author of *Overload! How Too Much Information Is Hazardous to Your Organization*, estimates interruptions and information overload eat up 28 billion wasted hours a year, at a loss of almost $1 trillion to the US economy (Schulte 2015). Having focused people in your life can help you become focused as well.

LEARN FROM AN ACE: WAYNA
During the interview I conducted with Wayna, we discussed how focus has showed up in her circle of friends and lead her on a productive path. Wayna started from humble beginnings, born in Ethiopia and moving to the US as a young girl. She would go on to stardom as a singer/songwriter and a few years ago had the opportunity of a lifetime: to join Stevie Wonder on his world tour. As a naturally creative person with ideas constantly flowing, focus is incredibly important to her in order to channel that creative energy and turn it into something productive.

Wayna mentioned how it is very natural to gravitate toward like-minded people: "It's a mirror; they mirror back to who you are and who you want to be or what you want to be doing." She went on to highlight someone who she admires, Mike Phillips, who is an amazing saxophonist but also a savvy businessman. She was intrigued by an endorsement deal he had with an athletic apparel brand that was paying him a year-long salary, which supplemented the music work he was doing.

While music revenue is increasing, a 2018 study showed artists only make 12 percent of music industry revenue (Bazinet et al. 2018). Secondary income sources can be critical for an independent artist. By being in Mike's circle, Wayna was able to humble herself and ask the simple question, "How did you do that?" It has been said success leaves clues and Mike was there to share his business experience with Wayna, which allowed her to then focus on her next steps to expand her business beyond music as well. Wayna has gone on to star in movies, sell custom clothing, and launch a real estate venture.

ACCOUNTABLE

"Accountable" starts with an A, but it should really start with "you!" While the ultimate form of accountability is what you hold *yourself* to, it helps when you have a friend or someone in your circle who serves as an accountability partner:

"A study by the Association for Training and Development showed the huge power of accountability. If you make a conscious decision that you want to achieve something, this increases your chances of success by 10–25 percent. Having a clear plan of how you're going to achieve it increases your chances further to 50 percent. But if you commit to someone else that you'll do it, there's a 65 percent chance of success. This increases to a massive 95 percent if you make a specific appointment with another person to report back on your progress" (Wissman 2018).

My good friend Toks and I have known each other for more than twenty years. We met at the University of Pittsburgh school of engineering and have been brothers ever since.

Whether it is a discussion on Sunday afternoon about our church service or a recent book we have read, our chats hold me accountable. Attending church and monthly reading are important to me (and him) so that accountability works to keep us doing what we said we were going to do.

CHALLENGE
When you speak with your friends, you should not hear a "chamber of echoes."

There is no growth without some resistance—resistance of an idea or action—that makes you think differently and perhaps take in additional perspective.

Considering a "chamber of echoes" helps you check your bias. It also helps you recognize the power of diversity.

If your circle all look like you, more than likely they all *think* like you, so the likelihood they will be pushing you or challenging you to think differently is slim. University of Arizona sociologist J. Miller McPherson discusses a concept called homophily in his paper, "Birds of a Feather: Homophily in Social Networks." McPherson defines "homophily" as people's natural affinity to gravitate to other people who are like themselves. McPherson notes, "Homophily limits people's social worlds in a way that has powerful implications for the information they receive, the attitudes they form, and the interactions they experience" (2001, 415–444).

In other words, when you're not being exposed to different types of people or points of view, you tend to be more closed off and less open to new ideas and opinions (Gordon 2021). Diversity of thought comes from diversity of race, ethnicity, sex, religion, age, and more. Just like a jet engine needs resistance in order to take flight, you need someone to challenge you so you can be sure you are staying sharp and prepared to soar.

LEARN FROM AN ACE: TOKS OYELOLA
Toks shared a recent example of a challenge I issued to him that helped him see a situation differently and come to a better solution than he would have otherwise. Toks prides himself on speaking the truth and practicing what he preaches. Those are core values he holds on to each day. He was in a situation where one of his dog breeding business clients was looking for a refund on a puppy. And while there is nothing wrong with issuing a refund, what Toks did not appreciate was the way the client was demanding the refund with a nasty attitude. Toks fired off at the client and essentially quickly dismissed his request and closed off communication with the client.

Later that day, Toks was explaining the situation to me and I could tell his decision to dismiss the request was not sitting well with him. He explained the situation to me and I could tell his decision to cut off communication with his client was weighing heavy on his mind. I asked a simple question: "How does this decision align with who you want to be at the end of the day?"

Toks realized the easy thing to do was hang up the phone and dismiss the client's request. When he got off the phone with me, he thought, "Now that is a true friend. He challenged me to do what's right." Toks proceeded to offer a refund to the client and explained to me, "The challenge was to not let me be or do something that didn't represent myself according to my truth and seeking to practice what I preach. You helped me do the right thing in that situation. That is the power of a challenge."

ELEVATE

Elevate is all about who is lifting you up. The world can be a drag and can get even the most positive person down. Without someone in your corner who is cheering for you and believing in you, it would be tough to be all you can be in life.

Good friends see the best in us and help us to be our best selves. They are our biggest fans and our biggest supporters. They are the ones who will always believe in us, even when we don't believe in ourselves.

I remember when my wife Shewit ran her first marathon, the Marine Corps Marathon in Washington DC in October 2019. It was a cold and rainy fall day, but we didn't let weather discourage us from cheering on our girl. Our closest friends and their children, fifteen of us in total, braved the cold, stormy weather and gathered around mile marker twenty to cheer. We were there with our matching "Team Shewit" shirts and just when she was about to hit that twenty-mile wall, she came around the corner and there we were, cheering her on.

That twenty-mile wall is real. Shewit was well aware of that challenge as she was progressing through the race.

Runners World gives further clarity of that wall, describing it as "depleting your stored glycogen and the feelings of fatigue and negativity that typically accompany it. When you run low on glycogen, even your brain wants to shut down activity as a preservation method, which may lead to the negative thinking that comes along with hitting the wall" (Susan 2019).

Shewit often describes that feeling of seeing all of us cheering for her as a "jolt of energy" that provided the fuel to keep her going and finish the remaining 6.2 miles. Your friends can lift you up, elevate you, and celebrate your successes, oftentimes when you need them the most. Your success is their success!

Those who are closest to you can often see things you don't even see in yourself.

As I shared in the introduction of this book, it's tough to see the label on the jar when you're inside the jam. When you are busy living life, it can be tough to see all the options available to you. Perhaps there is a talent you don't see or a new job waiting for you. You just need that friend to help you see it and make sure you are progressing forward with your head up.

I'll close this chapter with a story from my interview with Brandon Bowers.

Brandon has spent the past fifteen years in various leadership roles across large corporate organizations and he understands the importance of connection.

I asked him about a connection who has been instrumental in his success and surprisingly, he took that "mirror" and turned it right back to me.

Brandon shared that he appreciates my "passion for connecting with individuals in an extremely authentic way."

He went on to describe the small acts of kindness I do, which he said are huge acts to the recipient, such as going out of my way to celebrate someone on their birthday, documenting life stories through photo books, or sending a thoughtful text message. He also mentioned how much I prepare prior to a presentation, speech, or meeting, and how these lessons have taught him so much over the years.

I was humbled by this reflection from Brandon. This is the power of a Lollipop Moment.

What is a Lollipop Moment you ask? Let me explain.

Drew Dudley is a Canadian speaker, author, and educator as well as the founder and chief catalyst of Day One Leadership, an educational service provider that empowers individuals and organizations to recognize and create leadership every day. In his TEDx Talk titled "Everyday Leadership," Drew defines a Lollipop Moment as "when someone said something or did something that fundamentally made your life better." He mentioned we typically don't tell those individuals they have made our lives better (2010).

Lollipop Moments are those small, everyday interactions that have the power to make someone's day. They're the things we take for granted: a smile, a kind word, a moment of eye contact. But for someone who's feeling isolated or alone, these Lollipop Moments can make all the difference.

Drew mentioned that "it can be frightening to think we matter that much to someone else" and went on to make a powerful observation: "If we make leadership about changing the world, about something bigger than us, then we give ourselves an excuse not to expect it from ourselves and each other" (2010).

What Brandon's comments did for me was further validate that I am living my life in accordance with the ACES Pillars of Success. He wrapped up that portion of the interview by stating, "At the end of our lives, we don't know when we will hit that expiration date and what people are going to say about us. But I can tell you on that day, you will have a packed house speaking about you."

Drew explained, "We can have an impact on each other's lives far greater than money, power, titles and influence."

"We need to redefine leadership as being about Lollipop Moments: how many we create, how many we acknowledge, how many we pay forward, and how many we say thank you for."

Everyone has the potential to be a leader, because leadership is not about position or power: it's about connection. It's about helping someone else to see their own potential. By definition, leaders are connectors. They create a network of relationships that supports and sustains them. And those connections are what give rise to Lollipop Moments. It's that feeling of being seen and understood, of being valued and appreciated. It's the recognition we are all in this together. And when we feel connected, we are more likely to succeed.

STACK YOUR DECK

Think about your friends. Do they get in your "FACE"? Do they help you Focus, hold you Accountable, Challenge you, and Elevate you? As you think about "FACE," are there any gaps you need to address in your connections?

Go to www.StackYourDeckBook.com/resources to download the FACE Framework Tool.

When was the last time you gave someone a Lollipop Moment? Received a Lollipop Moment?

CHAPTER 7

Connection to The World

Every night before bed, I share three quotes with my two daughters, ages twelve and eight:

Life begins at the end of your comfort zone.
—NEALE DONALD WALSCH

Whatever you are, be a good one.
—WILLIAM MAKEPEACE THACKERAY

Never ever give up.
—JOHN THOMPSON III

At the heart of each of these quotes is a connection to something outside of yourself that is so strong it keeps you going no matter what is in front of you.

This chapter is about your connection to the world. In Chapter 5, we talked about the importance of your connection to yourself. Chapter 6 was all about your connection with others. In this chapter, we will talk about your connection to the world and how you can create a life you didn't think possible by reaching outside of your comfort zone to make connections.

To be connected to the world is to expand your creativity and options. By expanding your horizons, you allow yourself to explore new ideas and potentially find new ways of thinking about the world around you. You can explore different cultures and gain a broader perspective.

If we understand the benefits of connecting to the world, why is it so uncommon for us to do so?

It's funny how we humans operate.

EXPLORING OUR COMFORT ZONES

We like our comfort zones and feel nervous or uncomfortable when we venture outside of them. Yet, at the same time, we're curious creatures who want to know what's out there in the world. It's a bit of a paradox, but it helps to explain why so many of us choose to stay connected to the world through social media and other forms of technology.

Research suggests 58.4 percent of the world's population uses social media. The average daily usage is two hours and twenty-seven minutes (Chaffey 2022). In some ways, social media allows us to have the best of both worlds. We can stay curious about what's happening without having to leave our comfort zones.

Let's explore what can happen when we do leave our comfort zone and foster a stronger connection with the world. We'll do this by examining someone whose technology connected individuals around the world: Steve Jobs.

Steve Jobs gave an inspiring graduation speech at Stanford University in 2005 that has now been viewed more than 40 million times on YouTube (2008). Steve's speech was simple, centering on three stories from his life. I find his first story incredibly intriguing and I carry these lessons with me in how I approach life.

The story dates back to Steve's freshman year at Reed College in the fall of 1972. After only a few months on campus, Steve had grown bored with college and knew the classes he was taking weren't for him. He decided to drop out, but while he was on campus for another eighteen months, he proceeded to sit in on classes that piqued his interest.

One such class was a calligraphy class. Steve was intrigued by the typeface on the posters and labels on drawers, and although he didn't know it at the time, Reed was one of the top calligraphy schools in the country. He learned about different fonts, serif and sans serif, spacing, and what makes great typography great. He found the class fascinating but it had absolutely no relevance to his life at the time.

Fast forward ten years and Steve was in the design room with the Mac team discussing how to incorporate the font, spacing, typeface options into their new design. In this moment, Steve realized the calligraphy class was what gave him an appreciation for the typeface options they were incorporating into the new Mac. This moment changed the course of personal computers as all future versions had options allowing the user to customize their fonts/typeface on their documents.

Steve shared an important lesson:

"You can't connect the dots looking forward, you can only connect them looking backward. The key is to have the trust the dots will connect in the future" (2008).

You've got to trust something whether it's your gut, karma, intuition, or God. You have to believe the dots will connect in the future, even though we can't see the full picture yet. This will give you the confidence to follow your heart when it leads you off the well-worn path.

This is definitely true in my own life. Many of the most important decisions I've made have been based on faith by stepping outside of my comfort zone. And often, it's only in hindsight I can see how all the dots connected. But without that initial leap, I would never have gotten to where I am today.

STEPPING OUT OF A COMFORT ZONE

During my undergrad years at the University of Pittsburgh, it was not uncommon for engineering students to spend all their days and evenings in the building. The vending machines provided lunch so there really wasn't a need to leave. While I enjoyed my engineering classes, I learned early on the importance of exploring my interests outside of the Benedum Hall engineering building. I wanted to learn about other cultures, other students, and other majors so I could be a fully rounded individual.

One of my interests was fashion and music. I was intrigued by the styles from the 70s, most likely because I grew up in a house with parents who were hippies in the 60s and 70s; my dad even attended Woodstock Music Festival. I would always hear stories about my father's big afro, bell bottoms, and butterfly collars and my mom's long hair with flowers weaved into a headband. So when I left Benedum one day and saw a sign-up sheet at the Student Union for a 70s-style fashion show, I was all in!

Even though I was just a freshman, new to the campus and trying to find my way, I stepped out of my comfort zone and signed up to be a model in the fashion show. One scene was going to be all women and they needed one guy to crawl out on stage with a shirt off and be led out on a leash and dog collar by one of the ladies. None of the guys raised their hands and I can still hear them now: "Uh-uh, no way. I'm not doing that! I'm not looking like a fool!" Just then, I got that nudge from those butterflies in my stomach that want me to stay comfortable. I knew there was excitement on the other side of that fear. Should I retreat to my corner, keep my head down, and ignore the push, or should I honor that nudge and my curiosity and raise my hand?

I decided to do it. I went from being an unknown freshman to "the guy who crawled on stage in the fashion show." But more than that, I became someone who consistently put myself out there in the face of potential discomfort.

So how did these dots connect for me? It turns out, I would go on to participate in fashion shows all throughout my undergrad years and even did some parttime runway shows over the summers with a modeling troop.

In addition, as I mentioned earlier, I became President of National Society of Black Engineers. The fundraisers we held for our chapter programs included fashion shows I coordinated and modeled in. This also got me better connected across the campus with other student organizations, students, and outside companies who sponsored our events.

Being connected to a world outside of my engineering comfort zone provided a wealth of opportunities I wouldn't have otherwise experienced.

As I reflect on my leadership journey, it was my NSBE leadership experience that formed the foundation for how I lead today. In fact, I was recognized at graduation with the Engineering Student Leader Award and presented a University of Pittsburgh gold watch, which I gave to my grandfather, my role model, for his support and sacrifice delivering weekly groceries to my dorm all throughout my college years. Talk about a proud moment. And it all started with that first 70s fashion show that taught me how to push past my comfort zone and express myself in a creative manner.

ALIGNMENT OF CONNECTION AND CREATIVITY

Connection and creativity are often seen as two separate concepts, but they are actually deeply intertwined. Connection is the act of bringing two or more things together while creativity is the ability to see new possibilities and find new solutions (2022). Connection is the foundation of creativity: without connection, there would be no new ideas or perspectives to explore. Connection allows us to see the world in new ways and discover previously hidden potential.

In 1995, Steve Jobs told *Wired* magazine: "Creativity is just connecting things. When you ask creative people how they did something, they feel a little guilty because they didn't really do it, they just saw something. It seemed obvious to them after a while. That's because they were able to connect experiences they'd had and synthesize new things. And the reason they were able to do that was they'd had more experiences or they have thought more about their experiences than other people" (Wolf 1996).

This lesson Steve shared points to one of his other philosophies. He talked a lot about avoiding shortsightedness. If you are going to trust the dots will eventually align, you must play the long game to allow time for those dots to align. If someone is doing something wrong, for example, rather than correcting them, Steve felt it was important for them to solve their own problem so they could learn from it. He would offer guidance, but not solve their problem for them.

He had faith that their learning would occur over time and they, as well as the organization, would be better because of this freedom to learn.

LEARN FROM AN ACE: MINA BROWN

If you want to avoid shortsightedness, it's important to know who you are and understand your connection to the world. Let's revisit Mina Brown, an ACE we met in an earlier chapter, as she shares how to reinforce connection. Each year, Mina comes back to a personal mission statement. Mina's sense of self-awareness comes from introspection as a young adult and re-evaluating her career at the age of forty-five. She checks in with herself, asking, "Who am I and who do I want to be in this world? Who do I want to be as a leader? Who do I want to be as a parent? How do I want to show up in this world?"

Mina wrote her mission statement years ago and now looks at it once a year. She always has the intention that she is going to revisit it, however, she hasn't changed it in more than twenty years. She calls this her "true north."

A personal mission statement is a powerful tool that can help you to achieve your goals and dreams.

By clearly articulating your intentions, a personal mission statement empowers you to take action and step outside of your comfort zone and connect with the world around you.

By definition, a personal mission statement is a concise description of what you want to achieve in life, specific to you and your unique talents and goals. There is no one-size-fits-all template for creating a personal mission statement, but there are a few key components that should be included:

1. It should describe your values and priorities.
2. It should identify the steps you need to take to achieve your goals.
3. It should be inspiring and motivating.

With these guidelines in mind, crafting your own personal mission statement can be an empowering and transformative experience.

Mina shared her mission statement with me: "My mission is to share, inspire, and nurture excellence in myself and others in such a way as to ignite greater joy and charity in our lives and the world around us."

Mina's mission has not changed over the years and has provided the fuel along her journey from corporate America into the world of coaching. As you may recall, she took this leap when she was at the highest point in corporate America as a CEO and CFO and went into a coaching industry that was in its infancy. Without having this true north of a mission to guide her, the temptation certainly would have been to stay inside her comfort zone in the corporate world.

I have learned we all have our comfort zones. Whether it is the neighborhood we grew up in, the coffee shop we always go to, or the people we surrounded ourselves with, comfort zones provide safety and security.

But comfort zones can also be limiting. When we're too comfortable, we're less curious and more resistant to change. We disconnect from the world around us and fail to see the beauty and opportunity that lie beyond our comfort zone.

It's important to step outside our comfort zones from time to time to rejuvenate our sense of curiosity and connection to the world. By doing so, we open ourselves up to new experiences, new people, and new perspectives. And who knows? We might just find our comfort zone was holding us back all along.

There are endless possibilities waiting to be discovered.

STACK YOUR DECK

How would you describe your comfort zone and how often do you step outside it?

What comfort are you ready to push past?

What are your personal values and how could you embrace these values to step outside your comfort zone?

Go to www.StackYourDeckBook.com/resources to download a tool to help you craft your personal mission statement.

PART 3

EMPOWERMENT, ACE OF HEARTS

The Light

I am here to guide you
With a light that shines so bright
Take my hand and together we'll stroll
Off into the night
Don't be afraid sweet baby
I am here for you
I'll make you laugh
I'll make you smile
This I promise you
We'll live each day to the fullest
In the name of love
We've been given a gift
A gracious gift from above
—John Thompson III

I read this poem to my wife during our wedding vow exchange.

There is a light that shines inside of each one of us. It is a beacon of hope and empowerment, leading us towards our dreams and aspirations. When we allow that light to guide us, we open ourselves up to limitless possibilities. We become confident in our abilities and believe in our own power to create change.

The light inside of us is a reminder that we are each capable of greatness. It shines brightest when we pursue our passions and stand up for what we believe in. You are never alone when you have the light inside of you to guide you forward.

Are you ready to let your light shine brightly and use it to illuminate the path ahead?

CHAPTER 8

Confidence to Freedom

What do you think of when you hear the word "empowerment"?

Cambridge Dictionary defines empowerment as "the process of giving a group of people more freedom or rights" (2022). While I agree with this definition in principle, I would like to offer an alternate interpretation: "Giving a group of people [power]" requires someone else to "give." However, for our purposes, I want you to think of empowerment as giving to yourself.

The root of empower "comes from the Old French prefix 'en-' meaning 'in, into' and the root 'power' which comes from the early 1300s, meaning 'ability, strength, might'" (2022). The root, therefore, tells us the true meaning of empowerment: we need to look inside to our strength, our ability, our might.

Think back to the Attitude section and the importance of focusing on what we can control. If we are waiting for someone else to empower us, we could be waiting a long time. This may lead to waiting for something to happen in our lives or for our purpose or passion to find us. If we are going to make something of our life, we need to recognize the control we have over how it unfolds.

I've associated empowerment with the ace of hearts. The heart is at the center of empowerment because your heart is all-knowing.

Leading your life from your heart, a place of love with love, requires you to be in touch with who you are and what you want out of life.

What does empowerment mean to you?

To me, empowerment is about leading from your heart and following your passion. It's about having the freedom to be who you are without apologies. It's about living life on your own terms and trusting your own instincts. And it's about having the confidence to speak your truth and stand up for what you believe in.

Empowerment means taking control of your life and claiming your power within. It means knowing what you want out of life and being confident to lead with love. When you are empowered, you are in the driver's seat of your own life. You are the one steering the ship and charting the course. You are the captain of your own destiny. And empowerment starts with *you*. It starts with knowing *you* have the power to create the life you want to live.

Not only does the individual benefit from being empowered, but there are organizational benefits as well. A study of more than 7,000 employees showed that those who felt disempowered were rated at the twenty-fourth percentile of engagement while those with a high level of empowerment came in at the seventy-ninth percentile (Folkman 2022). Clearly there is a strong tie to engagement for those individuals who are empowered. As the study suggests, those who are disempowered also tend to be disengaged. Why is that so?

Let's explore some simple truths about empowerment, each of which explains why empowerment leads to engagement. These are mantras an empowered person might embrace:

We are strong, we are brave, and we are determined.

We know what we want, and we go after it with everything we've got.

We don't let anyone or anything stand in our way.

We are passionate and purposeful, and we make things happen.

We live our lives with intention, and we make a difference in the world.

We are the change we want to see in the world.

If you're looking for empowerment, look no further than your own heart. Lead with your heart, follow your passion, and watch your life transform before your eyes.

LEARN FROM AN ACE: DEANNA MOFFITT

An interview I conducted with Deanna Moffitt helped shine a light on the benefits of living a life of empowerment. Deanna Moffitt is the CEO of Luminant Leadership, where she brings her talents of coaching, improv, storytelling, personal development, and presentation skills to help organizations and individuals elevate their experience in life and leadership.

I immediately connected with Deanna as a fellow author and powerful storyteller. She is highly upbeat, animated, and engaging. As you will learn from her story, Deanna is a walking example of empowerment, but her life could have taken a very different direction.

THE PATH TO FREEDOM

"Is this all there is? Is this what I am supposed to be doing for the rest of my life?"

Deanna asked herself this after ten years as an IT Project Manager in corporate America. How many of us have asked ourselves those same questions about career or personal choices? Questions about purpose help us learn the importance of following your heart, claiming your freedom through the choices you make, and developing confidence in your abilities.

Deanna explained: "I remember sitting at my desk in an IT job I didn't particularly enjoy in Portland, Oregon. I would come in early, sit at my desk, and gaze out the window as the sun was rising up behind Mount Hood. It was a beautiful scene. I could picture myself as if I was standing on the top of Mount Hood and just going to take a step off. And I was soaring. I didn't know where the heck I was, but I had this incredible sense of freedom. That was the thing I wanted to feel and experience. I replayed the image in my head, countless times, and that was the thing that gave me the courage to take the leap."

Deanna left her ten-year IT career to pursue her high-school passion: improv comedy. Taking the leap and having the courage to pursue freedom can be scary but can also be well worth it. When we trust ourselves, we are able to step into our power and live life more fully.

We all have an inner guidance system deep down in our heart that is always nudging us in the right direction, but sometimes we get so caught up in our heads, we ignore it. This is when things start to go off track. Our head takes us in one direction but our heart wants something else. Our heartbeat gives us life, and not listening to it can have a devastating impact on how we show up in the world. But if we can learn to quiet the noise and listen to that inner voice—our heart—freedom awaits us. It is always there, whispering to us, telling us what we need to do. And when we have the courage to follow it, amazing things happen. As we will see with Deanna, our lives become richer and more fulfilling, and we find ourselves living in a world of abundance and possibility.

CONFIDENCE IS AN OUTCOME

Deanna's attitude toward life was grounded in a mantra she came up with: "I only have one shot at this life." In all she set out to do, she would strive to make it the best she could. As Deanna explained, "I saw people really stuck in their stories and their misery. And I knew there had to be a different way."

This "different way" and quest for freedom is what led Deanna to quit her job, sell her home, and move to Chicago to do improv at thirty-six years old. Inside the improv company doors, she noticed she was an outsider in stark contrast to the college graduates who hadn't been in corporate yet. Rather than embracing the idea she didn't belong and needed to go back to the comfort of the corporate world, Deanna drew upon inspiration from the Swiss psychiatrist, Carl Jung.

Deanna explained: "I could stay stuck in the [idea that] I don't belong, I'll never be able to do this space. People don't like me, I'm always going to be alone. I will never succeed at this. And this would have become my truth. When this happens, no matter what we do differently, we continue to be pulled back into this old story and behavior. We all tell ourselves stories and those stories drive our behaviors in life. It's like the quote from Carl Jung: 'Until you bring the unconscious to the conscious, it will drive you and you will call it fate.' So we all have these unconscious stories we often create in our childhood to protect ourselves. We need to identify those stories, claim them, and start investigating. Ask ourselves, how are they serving us and then write a new one. Until we do that, we will continue creating these patterns and not knowing what is wrong with us. That is the unconsciousness of bringing it to the consciousness."

I was intrigued by Deanna's decision to leave her IT corporate career for the world of improv. As an instructor fifteen years later, improv has become a central part of her business and life.

Deanna boldly proclaimed, "I think everyone should take an improv class. You learn how to be present as you can only reach to what is right in front of you. You really have to listen to people and value people's ideas and be able to follow someone else and also know when to lead. It has taught me I can go into any situation and be okay. [...] I have performed in people's basements, restaurants, areas that felt like back alley situations, and I have had the same attitude: we're going to do a show."

Deanna shared a powerful lesson about how improv strengthened her confidence, saying, "I've been fortunate from a young age to have the confidence to get up in front of people and speak up. The confidence of knowing I can handle myself in any situation is huge."

Deanna further explained:

> *"I have also discovered that confidence is an outcome. We get confidence through our actions."*

Deanna told me, "What we really need first to ever get to confidence is just a little bit of courage. The courage to step out onto a stage, sometimes in front of thousands of people and not know what you're about to say and create a show on the spot. That is an amazing feeling—almost like free falling—and you have no idea what's about to happen. You are so in the moment and some people would call that crazy courageous, but I felt like it was like a drug. You're completely in the moment and present and high to the experience. That is confidence. That is freedom."

Deanna's journey is made up of confidence and freedom and strongly rooted in her strengths. Deanna now channels those strengths to help individuals and organizations tap into their superpowers to experience more in life.

Over the years, I have come to understand confidence is not a superpower. It's something you earn by putting yourself out there, again and again, and learning from your experiences—good and bad. True confidence comes from courage. It's not the absence of fear, but rather the ability to move forward in spite of it. So often, we let our fears hold us back from pursuing our dreams. We tell ourselves we're not good enough, or we're not ready. But what if we decided to view our fears not as roadblocks, but as signposts? They can show us the way to empowerment and courage. Just like we heard from Deanna, when we are brave enough to listen to them, they can lead us to a life that is more fulfilling and authentic.

Empowerment is the power within. It's not given to us by anyone else: it's something we create for ourselves. And it starts with our beliefs. If we believe we're powerless, that's exactly what we'll be. But if we believe we have the ability, we can create good things in our lives. The first step is to become aware of our thoughts and how they're impacting our lives. As Deanna explained, what is the story we are telling ourselves? Are our thoughts empowering or disempowering?

Once we become aware of our thoughts, we can start to change them.

Empowering thoughts lead to empowering actions, which create empowering results on the path toward true freedom. It's the choices we make, moment by moment, that are key along the journey. We can choose empowerment or victimhood. The choice is ours and only ours. We are in control.

Deanna's story shows us freedom comes from within. It starts with empowerment: the act of giving yourself permission to believe in your own strength and ability. When you think empowering thoughts, you set in motion a chain of events that can lead to incredible results. You become more confident, more willing to take risks, and more likely to achieve your goals. And as you start to see the evidence of your success, your empowerment grows even stronger.

With each step forward, you inch closer to true freedom and to the knowledge that you have the power to create the life you want.

STACK YOUR DECK
What are some empowering thoughts you have at this moment?

What fears show up for you?

What actions could you take to confront the fears and help you build your confidence?

CHAPTER 9

Bet on Yourself

Sundays during the fall and winter months always felt like a holiday when I was a kid. It was a magical time of the year in Pittsburgh because Sundays belonged to the Steelers.

As the leaves shuffled across our yard and ushered in the bitter-cold weather, our family would huddle around the TV in the living room and cheer with pride for our hometown football team.

It didn't matter the opponent, there was never a question of who we wanted to win.

And while our loyalty was fully aligned to the black and gold, I always appreciated my dad's attitude with respect to the outcome of the game. Sure, there would be disappointment with a loss, but my dad always maintained the proper perspective when the boys lost, boldly proclaiming, "There aren't any Thompsons on the field." Then he would go about the rest of his day.

Dad believed that when the game is over, we return to real life, and we don't let the outcome of the game determine our outcome for the day. Reminds me of our lessons learned from the Attitude section: Event + Response = Outcome!

We would often have friends and family over for the games and his friends would often ask, "Thompson, how much do you have riding on this game?" to which Dad would respond, "I bet on myself." I recently asked my dad what that statement meant and he said, "No matter the game, no matter the situation, if I can't bet on myself, then I don't put my money down. I always trust me and my abilities. I bet on myself."

IT STARTS WITH BELIEF

No matter where you come from or what hand you've been dealt in life, you always have the ability to bet on yourself. This starts with having belief in your abilities and knowing you have what it takes to succeed. It's easy to get caught up in negative thinking and believe that you're not good enough, but you must rise up against these odds. It's important to remember that everyone has challenges and setbacks, but it's how you react to them that defines you as a person.

If you can believe in yourself, then you can bet on yourself, and that is the first step to success.

For many of us, it can be hard to find the motivation to get up, face the day, and place a bet on ourselves. We may not feel like going to work, working out, or even getting out of bed. One person who I have always admired is retired world class athlete and head football coach Deion Sanders. Every day he wakes up motivated.

Why?

Because he knows that there are people depending on him. As the head football coach at Jackson State University, he knows that his players count on him to lead them to victory. And as a world-class athlete and former Major League Baseball and NFL player, he knows his fans look up to him as an inspiration.

It's this belief in himself that has helped Sanders throughout his life both on and off the field.

WAKE UP MOTIVATED
Sanders' positive attitude and strong desire to bet on himself is something he learned from his mother while growing up. "My mother worked two jobs to make ends see each other…," he shared. "Seeing no one really come out of Ft. Myers, Florida, that was my motivation" (2022).

> *"I wake up trying to bless somebody, inspire somebody, encourage somebody, help somebody, motivate somebody, get somebody to the next level"* (2022).

"If you don't believe in yourself how will somebody else believe in you?" (2022).

And believe in himself he did. After excelling at both baseball and football in high school, Sanders was drafted by the Kansas City Royals in the 1986 MLB draft. He went on to play professional baseball for nine years before switching over to football full-time in 1994. Over the course of his NFL career, Sanders won two Super Bowls and was named to eight Pro Bowls. He remains the only player in Major League Baseball and National Football League to play in both a World Series and Super Bowl. He was inducted into the Pro Football Hall of Fame in 2011.

A NEW CHALLENGE

In September 2021, Sanders took on a new challenge when he was named the head football coach at Jackson State University, a historically black college (HBCU) in Mississippi. So far, Coach Prime, as he is known to his team, has been up to the task, leading Jackson State back to championship glory with a school-record-breaking eleven-win season in 2021 and to their first Southwestern Athletic Conference football championship since 2007. Under Sanders' leadership, Jackson State is quickly becoming one of the top HBCU football programs in the country, and is attracting attention and respect on the national stage. In fact, the 2022 season picked up where the team left off in 2021, starting out with a school record eight to zero start and a first time ever visit by the prestigious ESPN Game Day broadcast team for a recent game.

Coach Prime said, "We were truly victorious but that was not the highlight of the day. I think the highlight of the day is how we all came together as a people and supported college gameday. White, Black, Hispanic, Asian, all ethnicities, all social climates, all social statuses, and we did that. I was praying, praying, praying that God would not allow it to rain and storm so we could show America that we could show up and show out. And we did. And I'm so darn proud of Jackson, Mississippi. You have no idea. Just driving through the crowd on the way to the stage had me darn in tears just thinking about where we started from and where we are today" (2022).

"People want to tell me who I'm not," Sanders said in an interview with ESPN. "But I know who I am." And that is a man who is always looking for ways to motivate himself and others around him. Whether it's on the field or in life, Deion Sanders proves time and time again that anything is possible if you just believe in yourself.

You may be asking yourself, where does this confidence to bet on yourself come from and how is this a key to empowerment? At the heart of betting on yourself is a concept called *ikigai*.

FOLLOW YOUR IKIGAI
What is *ikigai*? In its simplest form, *ikigai* is a Japanese concept that can be loosely translated to "reason for being" (Garcia 2017).

And while that may sound like a lofty ideal, the concept of ikigai is actually quite down-to-earth. It's all about finding what brings joy and meaning to your life, and then pursuing it with passion.

While ikigai is often talked about in relation to work or career, it's really about much more than that. It's about finding a way to connect what you love with what the world needs, and then using that connection to empower yourself and others. It's about placing a bet on yourself, believing you have something special to offer, and then putting everything you have into making it happen.

In a world that can often feel chaotic and overwhelming, ikigai provides an anchor. And while the concept originated in Japan, it's an idea anyone can embrace. So whether you're looking for a new career or just trying to find more meaning in your day-to-day life, remember: your ikigai is waiting for you.

Ikigai is all about alignment at the intersection of what you're good at, what you can be paid for, what you love, and what the world needs.

What's more, ikigai is intimately connected to empowerment.

When you know your why, you're more likely to feel confident and capable. You have a sense of control over your life and your destiny.

Ikigai makes it easier to take risks and pursue your dreams. If you're looking for a way to bet on yourself, ikigai is a great place to start. It can help you find your purpose and fuel your drive to succeed.

My early days watching Steelers football planted the seeds for learning to bet on myself concept and it has become even more clear as I have observed the smashing success of many others who have bet on themselves. One such individual is rapper, producer, and fashion designer Kanye West.

I recently watched a Netflix documentary titled *Jeen-Yuhs* that chronicled Kanye's life and rise to fame (Simmons 2022). Let's explore Kanye's story through the ikigai lens and learn about the bet he made on himself that led to his next-level success.

WHAT YOU ARE GOOD AT

Success did not happen overnight for Kanye. His early rise was brought about through his relentless pursuit of what he was good at: making beats for other artists. Kanye's first bet was his 2001 decision to leave the comfort of his hometown, Chicago, for the New York hip-hop scene.

Kanye was starting to be known in Chicago, but New York—that was a risk.

What if he didn't make it on the streets of New York? How would he pay the bills? How would he stand out in a sea of others with the same aspirations?

Kanye's strong work ethic, often being in the studio around-the-clock, as well as his producing talent led to some early traction as the go-to producer for numerous top acts in the hip-hop game, including Jay-Z, Mariah Carey, and Jermaine Dupri. He went on to produce over 200 beats for other artists, including eleven top-ten singles and multiple number one albums (Fowler 2018).

WHAT YOU LOVE

Kanye loved making music and more specifically, rapping over the beats he produced. While he learned to bet on himself early, his betting skills were put into overdrive as he began to shift from being "Kanye the producer" to "Kanye the rapper." Musicians were starting to get comfortable with praising Kanye for his great production work but the vision he had for himself was far beyond the role of a producer. He went so far as shooting down people who said he was a producer-rapper by responding, "No, I am a rapper."

Can you relate to this pull Kanye was experiencing? He was good at making beats, and those who were aware of Kanye's talent could not see him beyond the producer label they had associated him with. As I think about my career journey from engineering to sales, across numerous industries and companies, and ultimately down the entrepreneurial path, these are many of the same challenges I was up against.

Similar to Kanye, several members of my family, close friends, colleagues, all had the same advice. They would often direct me to "stick to what you are good at." They'd say, "You have a good thing going in corporate America. Why jeopardize that?" As we discussed in the Connection section, it's important to have the right connections in your club and making sure your connections are keeping you Focused, Accountable, Challenged, and Elevated can make all the difference. Had I listened to those individuals, I may not have pursued coaching certification and launched my coaching company or written the book you are reading today.

WHAT YOU CAN BE PAID FOR

Kanye started doing beats but never lost sight of what he loved. Although he was failing to gain traction as a rapper, he continued to make his mark as a producer. While he was laying down the hot tracks for his artists, he was quick to hold a track aside for use with his own voice. Producing was paying the bills but rapping was his passion.

While his life as a producer was on the rise, it had become an uphill climb for him to be seen as someone who had potential outside of the traditional producer role. If Kanye had stayed in the "do what you are good at and can be paid for" space, the world may never have experienced those 140 million albums he has sold worldwide (Mendez 2021).

WHAT THE WORLD NEEDS

From his early days and humble beginnings in Chicago, Kanye always knew he was destined for greatness. He was so convinced that beginning in 1998, he had a friend of his, Coodie, carry around a camcorder and film his everyday life as he worked to make it onto the national stage as a music producer and rapper. Keep in mind this was 1998, just six years after MTV released *The Real World* on MTV, a reality show that helped usher in the reality genre that we have come to know today. Coodie was already developing quite the following as a comedian and TV host in Chicago, but Kanye was so convincing in his vision for the future that

Coodie dropped everything to join his travels and record the footage of Kanye.

How many of us would have done what Coodie did and drop all we had going for ourselves to move across the country with a relative unknown on the national music scene? Not many of us would. The latest findings from Northwestern Mutual's 2019 Progress & Planning Study suggest that when US adults face choices about how much risk to take on, most prefer to play things safe (2019). The tendency toward risk-aversion isn't limited to finances. The study also found Americans are more inclined to play it safe across many areas of their lives, including careers, where they choose to live, the activities they enjoy, and their social lives.

Howard Thurman said, "Don't ask what the world needs. Ask what makes you come alive and go do it. Because what the world needs is people who have come alive" (2022).

Why was it so hard for Kanye to drop the producer label or for other artists to see him as a legitimate rapper? One of the areas of contention was Kanye's style. The preppy polo shirt, popped collar, blazer, and backpack look Kanye was rocking did not look like many other rappers at the time. Ironically, not only has Kanye gone on to become one of the top rappers of our generation, but he has also staked his claim as a fashion mogul. In addition, *Jeen-Yuhs* is showing other aspiring producers, rappers, and entrepreneurs the power of betting on yourself. Above all else, Kanye was so strong in his convictions that he knew who he was, who he was not, and was confident in how he was going to show up on the scene as his authentic self.

Betting on himself ultimately paid off for Kanye as the years of producing beats for the top artists, making sacrifices to secure studio time on the backend of artists' time, and shopping his album around to different labels eventually led to Kanye being signed to Roc-A-Fella Records in 2002.

As Kanye has stated, "I believe in myself like a five-year old believes in himself. They say look at me, look at me! Then they do a flip in the backyard. It won't even be that amazing, but everyone will be clapping for them." He goes on to point out, "Nobody can tell me where I can and can't go."

The only limits are the ones we place on ourselves. Believe in yourself, bet on yourself, and then show up and be unapologetically you.

When it comes to finding career success and fulfillment, there's no one-size-fits-all answer. For some people, following their passion is the key to a happy and successful life. Others find that betting on themselves—taking risks and pursuing opportunities—is the path to fulfillment. And still others find that connection to their community and a sense of purpose is what really matters. Whatever your recipe for success, one thing is clear: bet on yourself. Pursue what makes you happy and don't let anyone else tell you what you should or shouldn't do. Embrace the power you have within.

Betting on yourself requires courage and faith, but it is so worth it because it shows that you are willing to invest in your own future. Never give up on yourself or your dreams, and always remember that you have the power to create your own destiny. Believe in yourself, place a bet on yourself, and watch as you soar to new heights.

STACK YOUR DECK

What is a bet you can place on yourself?

What are you good at?

What do you love?

What can you be paid for?

What does the world need?

Go to www.StackYourDeckBook.com/resources for a tool to help you find your ikigai.

CHAPTER 10

Path to Purpose

I have walked at least five miles a day, every day, for close to three years. No matter the weather or where I am that day, by the time my head hits the pillow at night, I will have logged at least five miles that day.

It all started in the summer of 2019. I purchased a Fitbit activity tracker with the goal of improving my physical activity. Being a data person, I quickly noticed a trend that I could not walk ten thousand steps (approximately five miles) for more than five days in a row. As someone who suffers from plantar fasciitis, a heal pain that is caused by inflammation of the tissue that connects the heel bone to the toes, I had always told myself I was not a fan of walking long distances by choice (Mayo Clinic 2022).

For more than a month, I would log five consecutive days of 10,000 steps and then, like clockwork, it would be followed by a day or two of inactivity, typically in the 5,000 to 6,000 step range. At the root of this limiting belief was the thought I needed to give my feet a break to avoid a painful plantar fasciitis flare up.

In September of that summer, with just under thirty days to my birthday, I decided to challenge myself to walk five miles a day, every day, up to my birthday. I wanted to give myself the gift of good shape.

Two and a half years later, I am still doing those five mile walks. And while my initial intention was to improve my physical activity, I soon found that those walks impacted all the areas of my life, just like finding your ikigai can do for you.

In their 2016 book *Ikigai: The Japanese Secret to a Long and Happy Life*, authors Hector Garcia and Francesc Miralles share ten rules of ikigai. These rules can empower readers to find their own ikigai and live a life of purpose. What amazes me is how one simple five mile a day walk presents itself in each of the author's ten recommendations from taking it slow, to spending time in nature, to being more active, and more.

Finding your ikigai can be a lifelong journey, but it's worth it to live a life of purpose. The authors write:

> *"Empowerment comes from within. It starts with accepting yourself for who you are and believing in your own abilities."*

When you empower yourself to follow your ikigai, you'll find true happiness and fulfillment. These ten rules provide valuable guidance for anyone seeking to find their purpose. Let's explore these rules the two authors have outlined and I'll provide some additional context to consider as you work to discover your own path toward empowerment and happiness.

THE TEN RULES OF IKIGAI

1. STAY ACTIVE; DON'T RETIRE.

The global population is aging rapidly. It is estimated that 21 percent of the population will be over sixty by 2050 (2022).

Conventional wisdom suggests retirement is a time to take it easy, kick back, and enjoy a slower pace. But recent research suggests this may not be the best approach for everyone. In fact, staying active and engaged in later life can have some significant benefits. Studies show exercise reduces the risk of early death, helps control weight, and lowers the risk of heart disease, stroke, type 2 diabetes, depression, some types of cancer, anxiety disorders, cognitive decline, and hip fractures. It can help improve sleep, memory, concentration, and mood (Hellmich 2014).

It can help to keep your mind sharp and prevent cognitive decline. It can also lead to a higher quality of life, increased feelings of empowerment, and a greater sense of purpose. If you're nearing retirement age, don't feel like you have to give up all your hobbies and pursuits just because you're no longer working fulltime. Instead, consider ways to stay active and engaged in ways that are meaningful to you. You just might find retirement is more fulfilling than you ever thought possible.

2. TAKE IT SLOW.

In a world that is always rushing, it can be hard to remember to take it slow. The pace of modern life can be overwhelming, and it's all too easy to get caught up in the rat race. However, there are many benefits to slowing down and taking time to appreciate the simple things in life.

Kimi Werner explains this in her TEDx Talk, "When you feel the need to speed up, slow down." Slowing down allows you to be calm enough that you can make good decisions (Werner 2014).

Werner is a national champion free diver, and taking it slow is what helped her complete the best dives of her career. Werner shared the importance of slowing down in the water, as speeding up takes more energy and raises your heart rate, and you can quickly burn through all the oxygen you stored up from the single breath of air you took at the surface.

Werner discussed a frightening encounter she had with a great white shark and how her deliberately slow approach enabled her to think clearly. Rather than frantically swimming away, Werner decided to calmly swim toward the shark, which ultimately slowed the shark down as well, and she was able to hold onto the shark as they swam in unison. She then eased away toward safety.

When you take things slow, you have a chance to think more clearly and reflect on what brings you joy and what gives your life meaning. So next time you feel like you're being pulled in a million different directions or find yourself quick to panic or act in haste, take a step back and remember to take it slow. You might just find that it's the best way to live.

3. DON'T FILL YOUR STOMACH.

It's a common saying we shouldn't stuff ourselves with food, but why? Is it because we'll get fat? Or is there something more to it? According to the concept of ikigai, one of the keys to a happy and fulfilling life is eating just until you're 80 percent full. The idea is by not overeating, you'll leave room for other things that are important to you, like your passions and relationships.

Research seems to back up this claim: a study from Brigham Young University found those who ate until they were only moderately full had lower BMIs and were happier than those who indulged in every last bite (2005). So next time you're ready to reach for seconds, remember: your stomach isn't the only thing that benefits from moderation.

4. SURROUND YOURSELF WITH GOOD FRIENDS.

Surround yourself with good friends and you'll be on the path to success. We went deep into the importance of good friends in the Connection section. But what exactly qualifies as a "good friend"?

Well, that depends on what you're looking for in a friend. If you want someone who will always have your back, look for a supportive friend. If you need someone to help you make tough decisions, find a wise friend. And if you're just looking for someone to have a good time with, look for a fun-loving friend. No matter what kind of friend you're looking for, there's sure to be someone out there who fits the bill. So don't settle for anything less than the best; surround yourself with good friends and you'll be on your way to a more meaningful life.

5. GET IN SHAPE FOR YOUR NEXT BIRTHDAY.
This call to action is one with a timeline and resonates strongly with me because I took this same approach with my five mile a day walking journey. Whether your next birthday is in three hundred days, one hundred days, or ten days, the idea is for you to start today. We all know that getting in shape can be tough. There's the whole finding time to work out thing, and then there's the actually working out part. And let's not even get started on the guilt that comes with skipping a workout or eating that extra slice of cake.

But despite all the challenges, getting in shape is worth it. Not only does it have physical benefits, but older adults who exercised regularly were more likely to report a sense of purpose in their lives, according to a study published April of 2021 in the *Journal of Behavioral Medicine* (Yemiscigil 2021).

Think about it this way: every time you work out, you're accomplishing something. Every time you resist the urge to eat unhealthy food, you're making a positive choice for your body. These small victories can add up to big changes over time, and they can give you a sense of empowerment that extends beyond the gym. So if you're looking for a way to get in shape and add some meaning to your life, consider getting started on your fitness journey today. It just might be the best decision you ever make.

6. SMILE.

Smiling is one of the simplest and most effective ways to live in the present moment. When we smile, we are sending a message to our brain that everything is okay. This signal of safety allows us to relax and be more present. Smiling also has a positive effect on the people around us. It's contagious, and it can help to create a more positive and supportive environment. Smiling has been shown to reduce stress, improve your mood, and even boost your immune system (Spector 2017).

So next time you find yourself feeling stressed or overwhelmed, take a deep breath and smile. It's a simple way to bring more peace and joy into your life and the world around you.

7. RECONNECT WITH NATURE.

The average person spends 90 percent of their time indoors according to a study by the Environmental Protection Agency (2022). And it's not just the typical office worker or city-dweller who's guilty of this; even those who live in rural areas spend the majority of their time inside. With so much of our lives spent indoors, it's no wonder so many people feel disconnected from nature.

Luckily, there are plenty of easy ways to reconnect with the natural world. One way is to simply spend more time outside.

Make a point of going for a walk in the park every day or spend your lunch break sitting on a bench in the sun. If you can't get outside as often as you'd like, bring nature inside by keeping houseplants or decorating your home with natural materials like wood and stone. You could also try reconnecting with nature through your hobbies; for example, join a hiking club or take up gardening.

By making a conscious effort to reconnect with nature, you can boost your physical and mental health and find a greater sense of purpose in life.

8. GIVE THANKS.
We live in a world of abundance. There is so much to be thankful for, yet often we take it all for granted. It's only when we stop to give thanks that we truly appreciate all the good things in our lives.

Gratitude is more than just a feeling of appreciation. When you're thankful for what you have, it naturally follows that you want to give back and make the world a better place. There is also scientific evidence that gratitude works. When we feel gratitude, the parts of the brain that are activated include the anterior cingulate cortex and medial prefrontal cortex (Fox et al 2015).

These areas are involved in feelings of reward (the reward when stress is removed), morality, interpersonal bonding and positive social interactions, and the ability to understand what other people are thinking or feeling. Gratitude rewires our brain so we become more likely to focus on the positives in the world than the negatives (Young 2022).

So let's start giving thanks more often. For the little things and the big things. For the things that make us happy and the things that challenge us. Let's give thanks for it all and see how much richer our lives become in the process.

9. LIVE IN THE MOMENT.
Giannis Antetokounmpo, NBA basketball player for the Milwaukee Bucks, was asked during a 2021 press conference, "How do you handle your ego?" Antetokounmpo's response gives us a picture into the power of living in the moment.

"When you focus on the past, that's your ego. When you focus on the future, that's your pride. When you focus in the moment, that's your humanity (2021)."

Antetokounmpo explained that a focus on the past—ego—wants to brag. Focusing on the future—pride—manifests as overconfidence in oneself. Both of these tend to result in poor performance in the next game. Antetokounmpo's approach is to focus solely in the moment, going out onto the court with no expectations, enjoying the game, and competing at a high level.

It's easy to get caught up in the past or worry about the future, but we should live in the moment and enjoy what we have. This moment is all we have, so we might as well make the most of it. We can't change what happened in the past, and we don't know what will happen in the future, so why worry about things we can't control? Instead, let's focus on enjoying the present moment. We can savor a delicious meal, appreciate a beautiful sunset, or simply spend time with people we love. When we live in the moment, we can fully experience life and all it has to offer.

10. FOLLOW YOUR IKIGAI.

Living a life of purpose is empowering. It gives you a sense of meaning and fulfillment that comes from doing something you love and making a difference in the world. And when you're empowered, anything is possible. You tap into a source of deep personal happiness and empowerment. Best of all, good things start happening all around you. You attract abundance and good fortune, and your life becomes better and more joyful.

Garcia and Miralles explain:

> *"There is a passion inside you, a unique talent that gives meaning to your days and drives you to share the best of yourself until the very end"* (Allan 2018).

We'll explore how to uncover that talent, or strength, which forms the foundation of the Strength section in the next chapter.

STACK YOUR DECK

Which of these ten rules resonated most strongly with you? Why?

Which of these rules present the biggest challenge to you? Why?

What is one action you could take today that aligns with these rules?

PART 4

STRENGTH, ACE OF DIAMONDS

Count It All Joy

All that plotting and scheming
Should have been used for a different cause
You tried to tear me down
But your plan was full of flaws
I do applaud your effort
Your plan took careful crafting
Looking back now
Who's the one that's laughing
When I think about your plot
It chills me to the bone
The very trap you set
Turned out to be your own
—John Thompson III

Adversity is often seen as a negative force and something that makes our lives more difficult. However, adversity can also be a great source of strength. It forces us to confront our challenges and to grow in the face of them. Without adversity, we would never know how strong we truly are. Adversity is not happening *to* us, it's happening *for* us. It's giving us the opportunity to become the best versions of ourselves.

Are you ready to rise up in the face of adversity and show the world what you're made of? It's time to embrace it and use it to make yourself even stronger.

The pages ahead will give you some perspective and tools to fall back on during those times of great challenge. You'll learn how to leverage your strengths, how to persevere in your valley, and how to ultimately transform your environment.

CHAPTER 11

Leverage Your Strengths

There is no more effective way to empower people than to see each other in terms of his or her strengths.
—DON CLIFTON, AUTHOR OF THE CLIFTONSTRENGTHS ASSESSMENT AND FATHER OF STRENGTHS PSYCHOLOGY

Diamond is the hardest natural material on Earth (Hussain 2022). Diamonds are formed deep within the Earth's mantle under conditions of extreme heat and pressure. This makes them unique among minerals and gives them their strength and durability. Diamonds have been used for centuries as symbols of power and invincibility. They are also associated with love and commitment, as they are very difficult to break. Diamonds are a reminder that we are all strong enough to withstand adversity. And like diamonds, we all have a little bit of sparkle inside of us.

In this chapter we will explore this idea of that sparkle inside of us that allows us to stand strong in the face of great challenge and adversity.

You can have the best attitude, build strong connections, and take ownership of your life through your empowerment; however, we know there are going to be those challenging events in life that test our faith.

Those events could knock us off track and maybe even have us question the track we are on in the first place.

THE TEST

In the summer of 2018, I experienced something that ultimately led me to the teachings of Strengths pioneer Don Clifton. I was at a crossroads in my life and wanted to do and be more. I was on a quest to follow my own heart toward a more fulfilling life. After nearly twenty years in corporate America, my career was a success by traditional standards but I still wondered: Was I living up to my potential and channeling all the energy and passion inside of me?

The crossroads I mentioned involved a job promotion I'd decided to go after. There were seven other candidates and I made it to the final round of interviews but didn't get the job offer. After receiving positive feedback from all the interviewers, the hiring manager said I was "98 percent of the way there and needed to work on 2 percent" to get to the next level.

I had won numerous sales awards over my career and in fact, at the time of the interviews, I was a member of our company's President's Club as one of the top sales performers across the country.

I received this message, and it felt like a gut punch. Where could I find that 2 percent I was missing?

This brought me to the work of Don Clifton and an intriguing question of his: "What would happen if we studied what is right with people instead of focusing on what is wrong with them?" (DeWeese 2018).

LEVERAGE YOUR STRENGTHS

Don Clifton was a pioneer in the field of positive psychology. His work has helped to empower people around the world. The groundbreaking book by Tom Rath and Gallup, based on the findings of Don Clifton, *StrengthsFinder 2.0*, introduced the concept of CliftonStrengths and helped launch the Positive Psychology movement. This online test (formerly named the Clifton StrengthsFinder) measures the intensity of your talents in each of the thirty-four CliftonStrengths themes. These thirty-four themes represent what people do best (2022).

More than 27 million people around the world have taken the CliftonStrengths assessment to learn about and develop their talents (2022). Through his work, Clifton showed everyone has the potential to lead a fulfilling and meaningful life because focusing on your strengths can lead to greater success and happiness.

According to management consultant Peter Drucker, "It takes far more energy to improve from incompetence to mediocrity than it takes to improve from first-rate performance to excellence." We get the greatest return on investment by focusing on our strengths, not struggling to improve our areas of low competence (Cook 2014).

Gallup further backs up this claim by explaining, "People who have the opportunity to use their CliftonStrengths are six times as likely to be engaged in their jobs and to strongly agree they have a chance to do what they do best every day" (2022).

When we focus on what is right, what's working, and what we can build on, we're more likely to have an excellent quality of life. In fact, people who use their CliftonStrengths are three times as likely to report having an excellent quality of life (2022). Strengths-based living is not about ignoring the hard stuff or building a false sense of self-esteem; it's about facing reality head-on with courage and optimism.

When we know our strengths, we can find the courage to be vulnerable, ask for help, and lean into the discomfort of change.

When we use our strengths, we're more likely to feel happy, engaged, and fulfilled. We're also less likely to experience negative emotions like worry, stress, and anxiety (Asplund 2020). If you want to live a happier, more fulfilling life, focus on your strengths. You'll be glad you did.

STRENGTHS IN ACTION

I came across a story that helps further illustrate Clifton's commitment to Strengths and the power of focusing on "what is right with people."

Cathy DeWeese is a senior workplace consultant with Gallup who worked with Clifton after his firm SRI acquired Gallup in 1988 (CliftonStrengths 2019). Cathy has spent the majority of her thirty years with Gallup teaching, working with coaches, or coaching other people. Cathy told a story about what it was like to work with Don and his relentless focus on remaining grounded in strengths.

Don needed someone to work with him for a summer internship, and Cathy handled the interviews, assessed the candidates, and gave feedback to ultimately decide who would be the best fit. The time came to bring her findings to Don. She brought the extensive notes she'd made about every candidate. Don's only question on the top candidate was "What does he do well?" Cathy explained the candidate's career goals and motivations, but Don interrupted with, "What does he do well?" Cathy outlined his work style, work ethic, and grades. Don grinned, and for a third time, asked, "What does he do well?"

Cathy then responded with, "He leads well, and he studies well. He focuses on goals well and is a natural relationship builder" (DeWeese 2018). That was what Don was looking for. He understood when we leverage our strengths, we open up a world of possibilities. We can achieve anything we set our minds to, and we can create our own destiny. Our strengths are the key to unlocking our potential and living a life of freedom and purpose. When we are operating from a place of our strengths, it doesn't take long to get to full potential because we are already working from a place of natural talent. We are operating within our passions and our gifts.

When I was passed up for the promotion because I "needed another 2 percent," I should have instead focused harder on the 98 percent I did well and not trying to find or improve the 2 percent that was missing. Making the shift from a 2 percent to 98 percent focus and understanding my strengths led me on a journey of self-discovery. I became a Gallup Strengths Coach and a Board Certified Executive, Career, and Life Coach through the Center for Credentialing and Education, and an International Coaching Federation Associate Certified Coach.

Asking myself the question, "What do I do well?" led to me explore how my strengths could be aimed toward more fulfilling work.

LEARN FROM AN ACE: TOKS OYELOLA
This brings us to another story from our friend we met earlier in the book, Toks Oyelola. For this section, he shared a moving story of how he leveraged his strengths in a very challenging, life-changing experience he faced in 2016.

Toks' daughter, Eden (who this book is dedicated to), was a beautiful soul who left this world far too soon. At the age of five, Eden was diagnosed with glioblastoma, an aggressive type of cancer in the brain. While she went through numerous treatments, surgeries, and therapy sessions, she passed away at the age of six. Eden's light still shines bright on this earth and we remember her for her strength, positivity, and how she lived her life while she was here. She is the definition of strength.

Dating back to his college years, Toks' dream was always to climb the corporate ladder in the consulting world and make it to the top as a partner. He spent twelve years of his career with a top consulting firm, and after getting married and having kids, decided to jump to another top 100 corporate company. He was thriving, had a successful career, and then all of a sudden, life threw this challenge at him. He took six to eight months off work to deal with her surgeries and treatments and when he returned to work, he was let go his first week back.

Toks shared that that was "the most trying time of my life. I have a daughter who is sick, [and] my wife doesn't work so I am the sole provider. I saw my whole life flash before me." He described how he prided himself on being able to provide for his family and now it was his self-confidence that took a direct hit. "I was scared, but at the same time, I didn't panic. I didn't get desperate, but it did let me know I didn't have as much control as I would have liked in that situation. I was an all-star performer and thought I was untouchable."

ADVERSITY AS A TEACHER

Toks chose to look for the lesson in this situation, in the midst of this pain, he clung to a mantra:

> *"When something brings pain, what is the lesson I am supposed to learn?"*

This led him to examine his passions, his strengths, and his goals in life. Toks is an entrepreneur at heart and has always had a goal to run his own consulting practice. The first thing he did upon getting laid off was start this up. While he was putting the pieces in place, within thirty days he got a call from another top consulting firm with an offer he couldn't turn down. This offer allowed him to have the stability of a paycheck, and insurance to care for Eden, while he continued putting the pieces in place to launch his own consulting practice in the future.

Toks spent three years with the consulting firm, and then an opportunity came to him where he could finally branch out on his own as an independent consultant. He achieved the initial goal he'd had for himself to become a partner of a consulting firm, which happened to be his own, and he got a chance to fulfill another goal, which was to run his own practice. As Toks explained, "Had I not been laid off, I don't think I would have jumped at the opportunity to launch my own practice. It was different, it was edgy, it was risky, it was foreign, it was something I hadn't done before." But it was the pain he faced with being laid off that he never wanted to feel again. This led him to tap into his strengths as a consultant and budding entrepreneur to eventually move beyond this adversity to great success.

LEARN FROM AN ACE: BRYAN DURR

In a time when the news is filled with stories of natural disasters and human-caused tragedies, it's refreshing to hear a story of heroism that doesn't involve violence or chaos. In our interview Bryan Durr, a retired captain of the US Coast Guard, shared the story of a search and rescue mission that saved three stranded boaters in the Gulf of Mexico. What makes this story even more amazing is that Captain Durr didn't do it alone: he relied on his strengths and his team members to get the job done. By leveraging their individual strengths and facing fear head on, the team was able to accomplish what seemed impossible.

Bryan is now retired honorably after serving thirty years of active duty in the Coast Guard in the role of Chief of the Office of Logistics and Business Operations, as well as a C130 and H65 pilot. His story of heroism starts with the chilling words you may have heard at the beginning of an action-movie trailer:

> *"It was a dark and stormy night. We received the call that a stranded boater needed to be rescued."*

Bryan was serving on an Air Station in New Orleans on an H65 helicopter, which had a range of approximately 250 miles, with a crew of only three. The call came in around 11:30 p.m. for a sailboat stranded about 220 miles off the shore in the Gulf of Mexico. After receiving the call, the team jumped into action: they put on their gear and checked the weather, the fuel, the mission plan, and the map for the fuel stops along the way. They had enough fuel to fly to the site (approximately an hour away) and then hover on site for ten minutes. They would then need to leave to refuel.

When Bryan and his team arrived on scene, they found the boat dead in the water, its masts whipping back and forth in the wind. They found a patient on board in anaphylactic shock, non-ambulatory, but moderately responsive. She was there with her husband, son, and dog. The sailboat motor was down so they couldn't get the sails up and it was pitch black with the wind blowing thirty knots.

At this point in the story, we can visualize Bryan channeling his strengths as he hovered the helicopter trying to lower a rescue swimmer but as the boat rocked, the masts swayed violently. After two or three failed attempts to thread the needle and drop the swimmer on-deck, they decided to drop him in the water about thirty feet away and allow him to drift back to the boat. Just then they realized they had spent too much time on the scene. Low on fuel, they left the swimmer and headed to the nearest oil rig about ten minutes away.

At the rig, another helicopter was fueling up. Bryan reported they didn't have enough fuel to wait, so the deck crew pushed it to the side and Bryan landed on the pad with less than ten feet of clearance between its rotor arc and the other helicopter.

After refueling, Bryan and his crew made the trip back to the stranded boat. At the scene, the swimmer had packed everyone up. He dropped the woman in the water and jumped in with her. Bryan sent the hoist down to lift her up. They repeated the maneuver, rescuing the other two passengers, the dog, and finally the swimmer. Mission completed, they turned around and headed to the hospital.

"It wasn't until I was finished and handed the controls to the co-pilot and instructed, 'Take us home,' that I realized how stressful that situation was," Bryan reflected. "That is what we train for. It was just decisive action that we took based on our training. This is how we're going to do it and this is how it will get done."

I asked Bryan a question about fear to which he responded:

> *"Fear only comes into play when you are not prepared. The preparation provides you with the confidence in your skills."*

Those skills become your strengths you can fall back on in times of great challenge. Bryan went on to explain the importance of staying calm: "You will live or die based on your ability to stay calm and think."

Bryan also shared the unofficial motto for the Coast Guard: "You have to go out, but you don't have to come back!" While they don't use this "motto" any longer, the bravery this quote denotes is not lost on service members. This is just one example of how standing strong in adversity and working together can create something truly remarkable. Whether you're in the military or not, we can all learn from Captain Durr's example and work together to overcome any challenge we face. Thank you for your service, Captain Durr!

Everyone experiences adversity at some point in their lives. It is inevitable. What is not inevitable is how you allow adversity to affect you. You can choose to let it get the best of you or you can leverage your strengths to get through it. As Clifton illustrated, when you do what you do well, you give yourself the best chance of success. And even when things are tough, look for the lesson. As we learned from our friend Toks, there is always something to be learned in the midst of pain or challenge. Keep taking positive steps forward and don't let adversity get you down. You are strong enough to get through anything life throws your way.

STACK YOUR DECK

Have you ever been told or felt you were not good enough? Rather than focusing on what you are missing, how can you shift your focus to what you have?

What has been the biggest adversity you have faced in your life? What is the lesson in this adversity?

What are your strengths? Go to www.StackYourDeckBook.com/resources for a tool to help you discover your strengths.

CHAPTER 12

Through the Valley

Have you heard the expression, "I was sick and tired of being sick and tired?" I know it's a cliché. But it was these words I uttered to myself on the morning of October 27, 2018, that would change my life forever.

This chapter will be a bit different than other chapters. No guest interviews. No research. Just a personal reflection on a deep challenge I dealt with for many years that came to an abrupt head in October of 2018. Without this moment, I don't believe you would be reading the book in your hands today.

This single moment was a turning point in my life that unlocked a world I didn't know, or believe, would be possible.

October 27, 2018, was the day I decided to stop drinking alcohol. While I couldn't have predicted day one was going to turn into four years as of this writing, what I did know at the time was I was ready to take a break.

I have always believed what you do in your valley determines the height of your peak. This particular time in my life was a valley. I looked at what I had become and I realized I deserved better. My family deserved better. My friends deserved better. And most importantly, I was capable of better. Although I was never a heavy drinker, I could certainly hold my own and what would often start as one drink would end up turning into half a bottle of vodka gone, or more if I had friends over.

Alcohol began to consume me; it owned my brain. I associated happy feelings with "having a drink." After a meeting, on the train, washing my car, out at the pool, on the cruise, on the plane, on the way to the store, at the concert—wherever I was, I always felt I needed a drink in my hand. I didn't even know myself, or fun, without a drink. And while the drinking and socializing was of course fun, what was not so fun was the morning after. I would wake up with a headache, groggy, and spend the day lying on the couch.

I had no energy on the weekends to take care of the house and was even tired when it came time to play with my girls. It was easy to just lie on the couch and check out. In fact, while I typically wouldn't drink during the week if I was at home, on the road I would almost always have a drink with colleagues or on my own in a hotel. Even if I didn't drink while at home, I was typically tired and would often fall asleep in my chair in the early evening. I would also stay up late, midnight during the week and two on the weekend: my sleep patterns were clearly off.

SOMETHING HAD TO CHANGE

A few weeks after my forty-second birthday in October 2018, I was getting ready in the morning. I looked down at the counter where I had set all the pills I needed to take: vitamins, allergy meds, asthma meds, and antibiotics for a stomach virus. Over ten pills, and after I just went to the emergency room two times over the past two weeks because of asthma attacks. I thought, "Something has got to change!"

Michael Jackson's "Man In The Mirror" came on my playlist at that moment and the words about looking in the mirror and making a change struck me. I decided right then and there to make a change. I was not going to drink that day. One day turned into two days, two into three, and so on.

I honestly didn't think I could quit drinking. It really took a rewiring of my brain. The first real test was a Wu-Tang Clan concert in DC with my college friends about a week after I committed to take a break from drinking. How would I explain it? Part of the fun of hanging out with friends is having a drink in your hand and feeling sociable. I didn't know how I would tell my college friends I wasn't drinking. I was on antibiotics, though, so I had an easy excuse to use instead of explaining my new goal. I drank cranberry juice and, surprisingly, I was still funny and had a good time. As an added bonus, I felt great the next morning.

I also started going to the gym on a regular basis. Out with the bad habits, in with the good.

I was rediscovering myself. I had a new fire in my belly that led to me reading more, writing more, and being more present for my family. Overall, I was experiencing far more joy in everyday life, had more patience, and absolutely cherished my family time. I also picked back up with my spiritual quest and started attending Zion church regularly with my family.

THE ROAD AHEAD
Will I ever drink again? I don't know. But for now, it has been four years without alcohol and I am in a happy place at home with my family and at a happy place with myself. I am proud of the transformation I am making, and the positive signs and energy I am experiencing let me know I am on the right path. I am setting an example I can be proud of. I am creating a living legacy that is aligned with who I aspire to be. I look forward to the simple things in life and I feel like I am living slower. And in this fast-paced world, couldn't we all use some time to slow down?

Do I miss drinking? There are times when I miss the feeling of going to a hotel bar for a martini or grabbing a drink with my boys or stopping in a corner bar and chatting it up with the regulars. But in all honesty, I still feel like the same person, especially when I grab a non-alcoholic beer or my typical go-to drink: a club soda, short glass, with a lime. I am experiencing more highs during the time I'm not drinking that far surpass the high I received from drinking. I feel the energy I had when I was in my freshman and sophomore year of college before I turned twenty-one. I was focused then and I am even more focused now.

I'm taking care of my mind, body, and soul and the blessings are flowing.

POWER OF FOUR CS

Reflecting on the journey of sobriety, I am reminded of the power of the Four Cs: Clarity, Confidence, Consistency, and Creativity.

CLARITY

I now have the clarity to slow down so I can clearly see and hear the direction I need to go. We live in a volatile world, and there are so many distractions that can pull us in many different directions. Focus and clarity are key to blocking out the distractions of life and focusing on what is important.

CONFIDENCE

Clarity has led to the confidence to trust myself and follow my truth. It's funny. I was always a social butterfly, but I felt like I needed a drink so I could be my funny, entertaining self. And when I was networking, I still felt self-doubt and pressure to say the right things and connect in the right ways. Without alcohol, everything slows down while I'm networking and I find it much easier to nurture relationships, represent myself, and connect with others. I never would have thought my confidence would actually increase without alcohol.

CONSISTENCY

Consistency is the result of clarity and confidence. Knowing where to focus my efforts and believing in myself and my ability have led to being able to step forward consistently. I really believe I can do anything because I know how I will feel every day. I will wake up every day in a peak state because my mind is clear and I have energy. No more groggy, foggy mornings. I wake up with energy. From my diet to exercise to the work I do, I am fully in control of my destiny when I am consistent in good habits.

CREATIVITY

As a result of these previously described good choices, I am constantly in a space where my ideas are flowing. Only difference now is I have the energy to take action on those ideas because I am no longer controlled by alcohol.

I have a chance to get to know myself again. I can hear my own thoughts and the inspiration I receive from God, and I now have the courage to follow through. Recognizing how sharp and brilliant our minds are, I asked myself why I wanted to dull that sharpness by consuming alcohol. I am fully in control of my life and that is a gift I celebrate every day.

So why did I stop drinking? I was on the cusp of something great, something transformational. Two years after I quit, I founded my coaching company, Team ACES. A year later, I got certified as a Gallup Strengths Coach, followed by a Board Certified Executive, Career, and Life Coach, and Associate

Certified Coach from International Coaching Federation. A year later, I began writing the book you are reading today.

Again, what you do in your valley determines the height of your peak.

I did it for Shewit, who deserves all that I can give as a husband. I did it for my girls, to whom I want demonstrate examples of a good man and the true meaning of love. I did it for my family and friends, who deserve the best version of me. But most importantly, I did it for myself.

I have a new life—a better life, a blessed life—with a beautiful wife and two girls I adore, and I don't want to miss a thing!

I share this story because it is difficult to talk about strength without being open about the valley I was in when I was drinking alcohol. While I'm lucky this wasn't rock bottom, I was still able to use it to take an objective look at myself and recognize I wasn't living up to my full potential.

And without that time "in the valley," I would never have been able to appreciate the peak I am experiencing today.

STACK YOUR DECK
As you reflect on your life, are any bad habits holding you back from the person you desire to be?

What could eliminating that bad habit open up for you?

What is a good habit you could replace your bad habit with?

CHAPTER 13

Transform Your Environment

Where do you go when you don't get into your college program of choice? Academic bootcamp!

In the summer of 1995, while most of my high school graduate friends were enjoying their summer of freedom before college, I was headed to the University of Pittsburgh's Engineering Impact Program, also known as "academic bootcamp." The Pitt Engineering Impact Program was a program specifically for African-Americans to help increase the diversity in the engineering program. Some of the students *had* to attend the program, like me, and others attended because they wanted a refresher before college classes began.

I was not at all happy that I hadn't been directly accepted into the engineering program.

"Who are they to suggest I'm not smart enough?" I thought. I went to an excellent high school and had straight As in all honor's classes. When I took my SATs as a junior and scored a 1050, my guidance counselor told me that was a good score and I should be fine to get into college. I later learned the average score for admission into an engineering school is 1260 (TechPowered Dad 2022). While 1050 could get me into college, it wasn't high enough to be directly admitted into the school of engineering. Thus, I was headed to academic bootcamp where, for six weeks, I would take classes from 7 a.m. to 5 p.m. and study from 7 p.m. to 10 p.m. afterwards.

I made it a point to become the top student in that class.

I answered all the questions in class, studied the hardest, and even tutored other students in the evenings. I also met my first black friends during that summer program. Having attended a high school with only a handful of black students, this was the first time I had a chance to interact for an extended period of time with individuals who looked like me.

By the mid-point in the summer program, I had all As and a few Bs. I realized then I could really stand out amongst my peers if I got all As. I focused hard over the next three weeks and studied close with another classmate who also wanted to get straight As. Then the final report card was in: I got straight As in the summer program! I was ecstatic and truly saw the benefits of my hard work. My friend in the class also did well, her lowest grade being an A-.

To celebrate, we had a banquet for the summer program for our family and friends. I was honored to receive the Outstanding Student Award and a special recognition for achieving straight As. My family was so proud of me and even put an ad in our local Washington paper celebrating my achievement. Just like when I was a kid, I was still happy to report good grades to my parents.

Something else happened during that summer: I transformed my environment.

That's right. I entered the Engineering Impact Program, a highly stressful environment, which often felt like a pot of boiling water, and I was able to transform my surroundings. I achieved at a high level but I was also able to help others perform better as well. I realized I was indeed a force to be reckoned with on campus and my best days were right in front of me. The future was in the palm of my hand and, if I worked hard, I would achieve great things.

ARE YOU AN EGG, A CARROT, OR A COFFEE BEAN?

Jon Gordon is a perfect example of someone who has chosen to use his strength to help others. He is the author of several books on leadership, including *The Energy Bus*, *The Power of Positive Leadership*, and my favorite, *The Coffee Bean*. In his work, Jon helps people find hope and strength in the midst of adversity. He also teaches them how to use their own strength to help others who are facing challenges. Learning to "transform your environment" aligns closely with the lessons from *The Coffee Bean* (Gordon and West 2019).

It's amazing what a little boiling water can do.

Take an egg, for example. With just a few minutes in boiling water, it goes from being soft and runny inside to being firm and cooked through. The same level of change is also true for a carrot: a few minutes in boiling water and it becomes soft and easy to eat. But coffee beans are different. They don't change at all when exposed to boiling water. In fact, they actually thrive in it, becoming more flavorful and aromatic.

What does this have to do with strength and adversity? Well, just like these different ingredients, we each respond differently to difficult situations. Some of us become hard and brittle when faced with adversity, while others become soft and malleable. And some of us actually transform the environment around us, making it better for everyone.

Just like the egg, the carrot, and the coffee bean, we all have different strengths and weaknesses. And just like these ingredients, how we respond to adversity is determined by our own unique nature. When life gets tough, remember you have the strength to thrive just like the coffee bean in boiling water.

Embrace your uniqueness and use it to make the world a better place.

We all face adversity in our lives. Whether it's a difficult situation at work or a personal setback, we all have times when things are tough. But how we handle these challenges can make a big difference in our lives.

The same is true for individuals. When we encounter adversity, we have a choice to make. We can either let the challenge make us hard and brittle, or we can let it make us soft and mushy. Or we can choose to transform the environment, using our strength to help others who are facing difficulties.

LEARN FROM AN ACE: BRANDON BOWERS

In our interview, Brandon Bowers shared a great example of how he was able to transform his environment through the work he does as a Little League baseball coach. Brandon lives by the principles in one of his favorite quotes by Mahatma Gandhi, "Be the change you wish to see in the world" (2022). It's through this lens that he approaches his role as a baseball coach for his son's team.

While he loves the game of baseball, Brandon said the real reason he enjoys coaching is the impact you can have on others' lives.

He said, "You never know what is going on in the life of a young person." His team recently made it all the way to the championship game and, as Brandon put it, "they didn't win." I like the way Brandon said that. He didn't say, "We lost," he said, "We didn't win." You may remember the power of this kind of small wording change from our discussion on mindset.

It was a close game, one to zero, that ended on a bad call at home plate that would have tied the game. A parent had a video of the player sliding into home and should have been called safe, but the umpire called him out. Game over.

Brandon and the team were obviously disappointed, but rather than be bitter or hold a grudge, Brandon shared with the team:

> *"You will learn more from this loss today than you ever would have from a win."*

He told them, "We are going to lose as well as we win, hold our heads up high, and shake their hands with pride. We will congratulate them on the victory, and we will be proud of how far we have come this season."

Brandon and his team could have easily followed an egg into that boiling water and cracked under pressure. Or they could have been like the carrot, soft and mushy and held their heads down and walked off the field with a sulking feeling of failure. But instead, by keeping their heads up, celebrating how far they had come, being proud of their abilities, and looking forward to next season, the team effectively transformed the environment and set the stage for a strong run next season.

This is a heavy lesson for a team of nine year olds.

Words from Jon Gordon further cement the lesson from Brandon's experience:

> [...] Failure is not a definition. It's just an event. Just because you fail doesn't mean you are a failure. It's just a situation to overcome and transform. And it will make you stronger if you are willing to learn and grow from it.
>
> —GORDON AND WEST

Further exploration of this idea of transforming your environment leads us to the concept of resilience. Resilience is the process and outcome of successfully adapting to difficult or challenging life experiences, especially through mental, emotional, and behavioral flexibility and adjustment to external and internal demands (APA 2022).

A number of factors contribute to how well people adapt to adversities. Predominant among them are the ways in which individuals view and engage with the world, the availability and quality of social resources, and specific coping strategies (APA 2022).

One specific coping strategy we will revisit now is the practice of yoga. You may recall we spoke about yoga's benefits in the Attitude section when Brandon Bowers pointed out that he adopted yoga as a way to bring about balance in his life.

LEARN FROM AN ACE: SYEED ABDUL-RAHIM

Another ACE we interviewed, Syeed Abdul-Rahim, talked to us about a challenging situation he and his son Isaac faced together. Syeed recalled riding around in a car after learning of his son's recently diagnosed autoimmune deficiency, understanding he needed to define his role real quick. He knew he was going to be all over the place, and quite possibly in the way, if he didn't figure out what role he could provide for his son and his family.

This brought Syeed to yoga.

He knew the autoimmune deficiency that Isaac was diagnosed with affected his muscles and if he could get him to commit to yoga, through Syeed's teachings, it would make a difference in his prognosis.

He said, "I wanted to give him that. I got into yoga so I could give my son a tool so he could strengthen his body and mind when I'm not here." Syeed jokingly commented that his friends were all surprised because he "used to be the guy who drank scotch by the ton and now this big six foot two, 250-pound guy is doing yoga!"

His response:

"That's called growth bro."

He was able to transform his environment through action. Syeed learned he can overcome his adversities by having something to do. He was reminded of his childhood when his mom used to tell stories that would transport him to another world.

Syeed closed with advice to "find your strength." He knew studying alone was his strength, whether it was studying Hebrew, or business, or science. "Leave me alone and I can get it," he proclaimed. Syeed went on to "get it," becoming a certified yoga instructor and opening up his own studio, Roctide Yoga.

Just like the coffee bean in the pot of water, Syeed internalized and ultimately transformed his environment despite his challenging situation. Not only was he able to learn yoga, become certified, and launch a business, but his son is also thriving as he works through his autoimmune deficiency. I can smell the coffee aroma that comes from both of these strong men.

In *The Coffee Bean*, Jon Gordon writes:

"I want you to remember this lesson for the rest of your life. Wherever you go and whatever you do, remember you are a coffee bean, and you have the power to transform any environment you are in.

"No matter how hard things get, or how hopeless things look, don't give up"

(Gordon and West 2019).

STACK YOUR DECK
What "boiling water" have you found yourself in the past or are currently in?

What would it take for you to transform your environment?

What could get in the way of that transformation? How could you remove that obstacle?

PART 5

PLAY YOUR CARDS RIGHT

FREE

All throughout the years
I've been comfortable with silence
Don't ruffle any feathers
Don't speak on the violence
We were always taught
That someday will be brighter
What if I'm the one
Who holds onto the lighter
It's time to spark the flame
That leads to the action
Change will result
Then comes the traction
That someday is now
That someone is me
Answer the call
Set the world free
—John Thompson III

Bold leaders are not silent during challenging times, and we certainly face challenging times today. We need more leaders to step up and own their power. Recognize what it means to be an ACE and know that with great power comes great responsibility.

It has been my pleasure to travel alongside you through the pages of this book and my hope is that these words will help you take control of the power you already have and stack the deck in your favor.

From here, our interviewees will answer two final questions, and then I will summarize the lessons taught by the four pillars of Attitude, Connection, Empowerment, and Strength. Turn the page and get ready to play your cards as an ACE in business and life.

CHAPTER 14

Life as an ACE

Being an ACE can mean different things to different people. The final question I asked each of the interviewees was to define what it means to be an ACE. While their answers were certainly different, a few themes remained consistent across each of their definitions, such as "being your best self" and "giving your all." Ultimately, it's up to you to decide what being an ACE means to you. I hope these responses give you a starting point to come up with your own definition.

BRANDON BOWERS

I think an ACE is somebody who is willing to stand up and say, "What is uncommon?" I think an ACE is somebody who is genuine in their relationships and is always willing to create connection to someone without any expectation of a reward. I think an ACE is somebody who trusts in the collective, hopefully diverse, perspective and ultimately arrives at an outcome that is far superior to what one individual could. An ACE is somebody who isn't static; they view life as a journey and there will be many highs and lows and twists and turns. It's not about what you achieve or accomplish, but how others feel in their interactions with you. More importantly, it's about your impact on the world and leaving it slightly better than you found it.

What is the best advice you ever received?

If you don't succeed at first, try again. If we stop at that first failure, we cheat ourselves. Failure is simply a learning opportunity in disguise. If you don't view it that way and embrace it as a learning opportunity, you are likely to repeat the same behavior that led to the failure.

MINA BROWN

Being an ACE is being the best part of you. Being the best you that you can be means having a ton of compassion and acceptance and literally radiating love for other people. Being an ACE means being the best I can be and then sharing that love with other people.

What is the best advice you ever received?

My marketing colleague on my informal board of directors, Wayne, said "Do whatever it is people will hire you to do." I was a finance geek; people didn't know me as a coach. I started doing financial consultations but then I baked in coaching in every statement of work. This allowed me to force feed consulting into every engagement, financing, restructuring, budgets: they all got coaching. Wayne said, "Let your clients tell you what your niche is." It was a natural evolution and then the referrals started to come in from there.

SYEED ABDUL-RAHIM

Being an ACE is like having a card nobody else thought you had. It's all about playing a card nobody else thought you had. And maybe you didn't know you had it, but when you found it, you put it on the table. ACES are all about finding hidden treasures that have always been there. It just took the situation to manifest it.

What is the best advice you ever received?

Be yourself. It's simple. I don't have to be the nicest guy in the room. Let people get to know you for you. Don't try to be anybody you aren't. Don't get fooled by the imagery you see. When you are genuine, it can be contagious. When they see energy, people take notice; they want that in their life. Be yourself and be genuine.

WAYNA

By yourself and when surrounding yourself with others, an ACE is humble. An ACE is service-oriented. You'll want to surround yourself with people who are inspiring you to share and give everything you have.

What is the best advice you ever received?

It was from Tony Robbins: "Your identity dictates what you create in life." You can put all kinds of energy behind trying to create something but if you don't believe it, if you don't believe it is you, you will run in the opposite direction and it won't be accomplished. Many artists run into this; it's called artist self-sabotage. If you don't believe that is who you are or what you deserve, you will screw it up or undo it. You have to know who you are, believe who you are, and constantly reinforce who you are and what you want to create.

Not only will you not get in the way of what your work is building, but you will see all kinds of other innovative ways to get to that destination. Your reticular activation system will allow your mind to come up with solutions and the universe will bring you helpers you wouldn't otherwise have seen. It's based on who you are, not who you think others think you are.

BRYAN DURR

In order to be an ACE, you have values, ethics, and morals, and you have to be true to those things and they have to mean something. In the Coast Guard, our core values were honor, respect, and devotion to duty. This is how you live your life in the Coast Guard. I embody those things. You have to be a person of your word. You say you are going to do things, then you have got to do it. Whenever you do something, you have to do it to the best of your ability. Be the best you can every time so you are always presenting in the same way every time. People know what they're going to get from you. Those two things create consistency: consistency in how you interact, consistency in the products you produce, and consistency with what people expect of you.

Lastly, I've always tried to be a servant leader. I know I can't get anywhere near successful without my colleagues or the people who work for me. I am always trying to make the folks who work for me better. If I can make them better or more successful, then our overall product will be better.

What is the best advice you ever received?

Always ask for what you want. No one can read your mind. I learned very early in my military career that you will always be your best advocate, so don't be afraid to make your desires known and back it up with positive actions. You will be challenged to walk the talk but that's why you put yourself out there, right?

TOKS OYELOLA

An ACE, for me, is individual. I look at it in terms of just myself. And I would say for me, the moment my life started to flourish is when I began to look at life and make things very simple. What do I mean by that? We all search for purpose. But for me, it became very simple, very clear: be the best version of Toks I can be. The best version of yourself you can be. That's numero uno: that's the ACE. Every day I'm on this earth, every day I live my life, I try to be the best version of myself I can be. And that's really what I think of when I think of an ACE.

Sometimes you wake up and say, "I feel crappy today. I'm not the best version of myself. I got mad today." But that's really what it means to me, I'm the only ACE. And I should always strive to be that ACE. Some people will come and try to take you off your game or people will try to get you rattled, but that's my responsibility. And that's really, my purpose—being the best dad, best husband, best employee—comes with just me waking up having that attitude every day to be the best version of me. The best ACE. And if I can live up to that, it trickles down to all the people I touch, all the people I work with, the people I'm involved with, all the projects I touch, all the businesses I do. It starts with me understanding I need to be the best version of me for everything else to fall into place. That's why I like the whole ACES concept. I believe in it; I think we all need to be ACES.

What is the best advice you ever received?

The best advice I ever received was from my dad: "Don't worry, son. One day it will all make sense." This was a phrase I would go on to hear all my life but not until my forties did I truly understand what this meant. You can have abundant information or knowledge but until you possess the experience and wisdom to understand it, you will never be able to apply or use it to your benefit. Time is what allows us to obtain that experience and wisdom.

DEANNA MOFFITT

Being an ACE is like throwing down an ace at a card table; everyone is celebrating, it's a moment of winning. It's playing out your whole hand. Play it all out and drop the ace. When you know that card is in your hand, you know you can win. I love that feeling.

What is the best advice you ever received?

It's so simple. It's just keep going. Just keep going. If I just keep going, the path is gonna be laid out for me. And it can be really hard, especially in those moments when I'm feeling stuck and I don't know what I'm doing. I don't know what I'm doing here, but I just keep going and know I will figure it out.

MY DEFINITION OF ACES

ACES operate at the top of their game. They achieve at the highest level. They are true to themselves and always challenge the status quo. They show up to engage and perform at their best. Whether you score an ACE on the tennis court, an ACE on the golf course, or ACE an exam, ACES are synonymous with achievement. The highest card in the deck, ACES are the very best.

STACK YOUR DECK

What does it mean to be an ACE?

What is the best advice you ever received?

What is one action you could take to elevate yourself to the top of your game?

CHAPTER 15

Go Team ACES

Every morning in Africa, a gazelle wakes up. It knows it must run faster than the fastest lion in order to survive. Every morning a lion wakes up. It knows it must outrun the slowest gazelle or it will starve to death. It doesn't matter whether you're a lion or gazelle. When the sun comes up, you'd better be running.
—DAN MONTANO

Someone is always chasing after us. If you are going to reach the top of your game, it's important to recognize your competition is coming after your spot. Someone else is always working to get better, and none of us can afford to sit idle while this happens. Sitting idle is the easiest way to get left behind. Accepting things as they are and not pushing yourself to do better or get better is a sure-fire way of getting caught by the lions.

Lions are one of the most amazing animals in the world. Not only are they incredibly powerful and brave, but they also hunt in a unique way. Unlike other predators, lions hunt in a pride. They are connected as a pack, and they know who they are. Each lion has a specific role to play in the hunt, and they work together to take down their prey. It is an amazing sight to behold, and it is a testament to the power of teamwork. When you see a lion pride in action, you cannot help but be inspired by their strength and unity.

Lions are also powerful creatures. They recognize their strength and they carry themselves with confidence. They have a freedom many animals don't. They can go where they want when they want. And they do so with a sense of ease and power. Lion cubs are born into this world with all the potential to be great leaders. But it's up to them to recognize their power and to use it in positive ways. When lion cubs grow up, they have the potential to be some of the strongest creatures on the planet. Let's all strive to be a little more like lions by recognizing our own inner strength and using it to make the world a better place.

MY ACES JOURNEY

My ACES journey began when my friend Sarah made a simple comment to me: "Every time you inspire me. One of these days we will be watching your YouTube videos." While that day in the summer of 2018 ignited the spark in me to do something bigger with my life, as you have learned through these pages, that seed was planted at a very early age.

I've experienced the challenges of getting off the bus to the words "bye little n*gger," to being cut from my high school baseball team three years in a row, to the highs of gold medal performance in the high school academic decathlon, to the many awards and accolades in college and my professional career. Without the ACES Pillars of Success, I would not have been able to weather those storms of life with the grace, tenacity, and perseverance I live with to this day.

I have enjoyed this writing journey and, as with anything in life, have learned a great deal along the way. I'll share with you a few closing reflections along the ACES Pillars of Success:

ATTITUDE

Attitude, the ACE of Spades, is everything. It really is the foundation for success or failure in anything you do. You have a choice every day regarding the attitude you will embrace for that day. Regardless of the events and circumstances happening around you, you can control your attitude and you have a choice. People will respond to your attitude whether it be positive or negative. A positive attitude becomes a catalyst for action and combined with a growth mindset, the world becomes your canvas to explore. When you change your attitude, it changes your whole outlook on life which then propels you into taking actions towards success. Having a positive attitude is not only infectious but also creates an environment that attracts success. Be intentional about the attitude you bring with you into every situation and let it be the driving force behind everything you do. Everything starts with attitude, and the good news is you control your attitude. So make sure it's a positive one!

CONNECTION

Connection, the ACE of Clubs, is what keeps you grounded and on track along your success journey. Connection is what gives purpose and meaning to our lives. It's what we're all searching for. And the good news is that connection is something we can cultivate. It's not something that only happens when the stars align. We can proactively seek out connection, starting with connection to ourselves and then with others. We should remember to surround ourselves with people who we want to be like. As Jim Rohn pointed out, we become the average of our five closest friends, so it's important to choose wisely who we spend our time with. Another way to create connection is by being open, curious, and giving back to the world. When we contribute our time, energy, and resources to something bigger than ourselves, we create connection. It doesn't matter what form this takes, be it volunteering at a local soup kitchen or planting trees in your community. The important thing is we take action and create connection in our lives!

EMPOWERMENT

Empowerment, the ACE of Hearts, is all about recognizing you have the power within. No one can define you except for you. Empowerment is about being confident in who you are, being true to yourself, and celebrating your freedom. You are the only one who can create your reality and determine your success. Empowerment also means living your purpose and following your ikigai to a life of meaning and purpose. Empowerment is a state of mind that allows you to create the life you want to live. When you are empowered, you are in control of your destiny and nothing can hold you back.

Empowerment is the key to success in all areas of your life. When you are empowered, you can achieve anything you set your mind to. Remember you are the only one who can create the life you want to live. You have the power within you to make your dreams a reality. So go out there and claim empowerment for yourself!

STRENGTH

Strength, the ACE of Diamonds, is all about overcoming life's great challenges. We all face adversity in our lives. It's how we deal with that adversity that defines us. When we are faced with a challenge, we can either let it defeat us or we can use it as an opportunity to grow stronger. The choice is ours. If we choose to grow stronger, we will find our talents and abilities can help us to overcome any obstacle. Just like a coffee bean, we have the power to transform our environment. We can choose to be the victim or the victor. When we are down in the valley of life, it may seem like there is no way out. But if we remember every peak is preceded by a valley, we can find the strength to carry on. The clouds may block out the sun for a time, but eventually they will clear and the sun will shine again. So don't let the valleys of life get you down. Remember that by leveraging your talents and abilities, you can overcome any adversity and reach new heights of success!

HIT THE GROUND RUNNING

Now that your deck is stacked, it's time to own your power. You are now playing with a hand full of ACES, so appreciate all you have accomplished up to this point. Above all else, you have to hit the ground running every single day. Don't question your power. Instead, recognize it, embrace it, hone it, and run. Honor the journey you have traveled and recognize your best days are always in front of you. Wake up each morning knowing you are an ACE in business and life. Now go out there with your deck stacked and show the world what you're made of. Go Team ACES!

Acknowledgments

As far back as I can remember, I have wanted to write a book. The individuals listed below have been key to turning that dream into a reality. I call this group of individuals The 300 Club, in celebration of ordering more than 300 signed books during the thirty-day pre-sale campaign. Whether you purchased individual copies, multiple copies, coaching sessions, and/or professional development workshops, your contribution to this campaign is something I will always remember. You gave life to this book and this dream, and I am forever grateful for your ongoing encouragement, love, and support.

Syeed Abdul-Rahim
Tessa Abdul-Rahim
Isaac Abdul-Rahim
Omar Abdul-Rahim
Haddas W Abraha
Sara Abraha
Yohans Abraha
Dawit Abraham
Heather Afriyie
Phil Agbeko

Isabelle Agurcia
Josef Allen
Sara Amare
Kathleen Amicon
Johnathan Andrus
Israel Anifowose
Semhal Araya
Michael Aschenaki
Helen Ayenew
Michael Bailey
Nyia Barnes
Candy Barone
Sterling Barksdale
Carlo Batts
Yasmin Behbehani
Ivan Benson
Sheba Berhane
Jonathan Birriel
Eddie Bland III
T Boddy
JA Bonner
Matthew Bottone
Aliese Bowers
Alivia Bowers
Brandon Bowers
Coleman Bowers
Phylicia Brathwaite
Sheenell Brown
Mina Brown
Jennifer Burgess
Paul Burnett
James Butler

Christian Cabatingan
Angie Cardenas
Reginald Carter
Kevin Chadwick
Robert Cirvello
Kimberly Coles
Susan Collins
Kelly Conrad
Kevin Cooke
Lisa Cooper
Roberto Cotes
John Cranston
Brian Davis
Richard Davis
Malcolm Dennis
Alexis DeWalt
George Douglas
Caryn Douglas
Camryn Douglas
Daryl Douglas
Daryl Douglas Jr.
Mike Duncan
Jacques Dupre
Bryan Durr
Nia Eddie
Dane Edley
Alexander Evans
Tennille Foster
Ashley Francis
Patrick Gale
Arden Garnett
Eric Goldberg

Kimberly Garman
Shonda Greene
Jim Gute
Robin Guyton
Kristen Hajibrahim
Marriaine Hak
Pamela Hall
LaToya Hammond
John Hart
Tamara Herring
Kathleen High
Lou Holder
Karima Holmes
Anthony Horton
Braden Horton
Jackson Horton
Jillian Horton
Dennis Howland
Ed Howe
Teshera Hull
Alicia Hullinger
Chad Jackson
Charles Jackson
Marcell Jackson
Khayla James
Elizabeth Ivy Johnson
Wendy Johnson
Ade Jolayemi
James Jolayemi
Isaiah Jones
Corey Jones
Michelle Jones

Zhuri Jones
Kenya Jordan
Renzi Kidanemariam
Derrick Knox
Eric Koester
Michelle Landery
Sterling Leaven
Jackie Levin
Marcus Lewis
Darrell Macon
Kaamilya Major
Jeremy Malecha
Orrin Marcella
Kamille March
Leigh March
Kelly March
Thomas March Jr
Darryl Marshall
Nicole McCray
Daniella Menchaca
William Milton
Kimberly Mingo
Melanie Mixon
Ashley Mohamed
Melodie Moore
Chloe Morgan
Jack Morgan
LaDonna Morgan
John A. Morgan III
Delaney Mullen
Nicholas Ness
Ed Nweke

Ade Omitowoju
Ron Orcutt
Arthur Osueke
Nyala Osueke
Yemi Oyelola
Aden Oyelola
Sade Oyelola
Tobi Oyelola
Toks Oyelola
Barb Payne
Christopher Payne
Afiya Perkins
Brandon Perkins
Eddlentz Philistin
Nahdia Pirzada
Terry Pompey
LeRoy (Tony) Proctor
Reginald Riley
Karysse Robinson
Manny Rodrigues III
Helena Rudolph
Derrick Rumenapp
Danielle Ruttman
Tierra Ryan
Jillian Sanders
Kelly Scott
Brian Seales
Ashley Sharp
Isaiah Simpson
Memo Smith
Timothy LT Smith
Rodney Somerville

Ikeya Speed
Kyrke Stephen
Beza Stephen
Zema Stephen
Wayna Stephen
Kyle Stephen
Courtney Stoner
JA Stringfield
Ashford Summerville
Shirley Taylor
Connie Thames
Janice Thomas
Connie Thompson
John Thompson Jr.
Naomi Thompson
Soliana Thompson
Shewit Thompson
William Thompson
Ebonee Thrower
Mekdela Tirfe
Mathew Topping
Andrea Tropeano
Diana Tucker Harrison
Greg Turner
Chi Chi Udoye
Saundra Van Dyke
Brian Van Dyke
Melanie Varin
Tanya Vaughn-Patterson
Devika Washington
Stan Washington
Catherine Watson

Lisa Williamson
Rob Wilson
Sarah Wollenhaupt
Mene Zua

To the ACES I interviewed for this book, thank you for opening up and sharing your story with me and the rest of the world. It was an honor to spend time with you, and more than that, I'm proud to call each one of you a friend. Just as iron sharpens iron, I have no doubt your words of wisdom will help readers stay sharp and on the path to their next level of success in business and life.

Brandon Bowers
Mina Brown
Bryan Durr
Deanna Moffitt
Toks Oyelola
Syeed Abdul-Rahim
Wayna

Thank you. Thank you. Thank you. These are the words I am left with after thinking about the amazing organizations I have been a part of over the years. Each one of these groups has helped me to grow in some way, whether it be as an individual or as a leader. I am truly grateful to have had such positive influences in my life. Through these organizations, I have made lifelong friends. To know I have your support is humbling and incredible. I strongly believe in the importance of surrounding myself with driven, ambitious individuals. Thank you for supporting my book and helping me bring this dream to life. Thank you, from the bottom of my heart. Thank you.

African-American Forum
DC Strokers Golf Club
National Sales Network
National Society of Black Engineers
Zion Church

Writing a book can be a lonely sport. Late nights when the world is sleeping or weekends when the world is having fun were instead my moments to write. I would like to send a special thank you to the Manuscripts team, New Degree Press, and the instructors, editors, marketing specialists, and cover design team with whom I had the pleasure of collaborating over the past year. Thank you for keeping me on track and committed to accomplishing this goal. You all make writing fun!

Eric Koester
Shanna Heath
Kyra Ann Dawkins
Ty Mall
Haley Newlin
Erinn Kemper
Jacques Moolman
Sherman Morrison
John Saunders
Ethan Turer
Reilly Vore
Gjorgi Pejkovski
Logan Austin

I grew up with some amazing parents, grandparents, and family who always encouraged me to chase my dreams. They taught me the importance of hard work, never giving up, and how to live a life of service and impact. They were a huge blessing in my life, and I will always be grateful for their love and support.

Last but not least, I want to acknowledge you. Thank you for reading this book. My passion is to help others walk in purpose and inspired to reach their full potential. I believe in you, I am always rooting for you, and I know you have greatness inside of you. Onward and upward. Can't stop, won't stop!

Go Team ACES!
—JT

Appendix

INTRODUCTION

Fernstrom, Madelyn. 2019. "Dr. Fernstrom: Are you at risk for job burnout?" MSNBC. Accessed October 24, 2022. https://www.msnbc.com/know-your-value/dr-fernstrom-are-you-risk-job-burnout-n1039376.

Kelly, Jack. 2021. "Indeed Study Shows That Worker Burnout Is At Frighteningly High Levels: Here Is What You Need To Do Now." *Forbes*. April 5, 2021. https://www.forbes.com/sites/jackkelly/2021/04/05/indeed-study-shows-that-worker-burnout-is-at-frighteningly-high-levels-here-is-what-you-need-to-do-now.

Sharma, Robin. 2013. "Leading Without A Title." Talk delivered at IESE as part of the Fast Forward program. May 30, 2013. 2:53. https://youtu.be/u9IEeHqsTDs.

Von Herder, Johann Gottfried. Quotable Quotes. Goodreads. Accessed October 24, 2022. https://www.goodreads.com/quotes/425990-without-inspiration-the-best-powers-of-the-mind-remain-dormant.

CHAPTER 1: ACES PILLARS OF SUCCESS

"Amwell Township in Pennsylvania." City Population. Accessed October 24, 2022. https://www.citypopulation.de/en/usa/pennsylvania/admin/washington/4212502384__amwell/

Dweck, Carol. 2016. "What Having a 'Growth Mindset' Actually Means." *Harvard Business Review*, January 13, 2016. https://hbr.org/2016/01/what-having-a-growth-mindset-actually-means.

"Loving v. Virginia, 388 U.S. 1 (1967)." Justia, US Supreme Court. Accessed October 24, 2022. https://supreme.justia.com/cases/federal/us/388/1/.

McCarthy, Justin. 2021. "U.S. Approval of Interracial Marriage at New Highs of 94%." Gallup. September 10, 2021. https://news.gallup.com/poll/354638/approval-interracial-marriage-new-high.aspx.

Rath, Tom and Jim Harter. 2010. "Your Friends and Your Social Well-Being." Gallup Business Journal. August 19, 2010. https://news.gallup.com/businessjournal/127043/friends-social-well-being.aspx.

Sanders, Henry Russel. 1984. "Winning isn't everything, it's the only thing." Vanderbilt University football coach, c. 1948. Leo Green, Sportswit, p. 57.

Stallone, Sylvester. 2010. "It's all about how hard you get hit and move forward." August 24, 2010. 2:06. https://www.youtube.com/watch?v=44EROHumt4Q.

CHAPTER 2: WORK-LIFE HARMONY

"6 Ways Physical Balance Improves Mental Health." *FLUIDSTANCE.* August 4, 2020. https://blog.fluidstance.com/2020/08/6-ways-physical-balance-improves-mental-health/.

American Osteopathic Association. n.d. "Maintaining a regular yoga practice can provide physical and mental health benefits." Accessed October 24, 2022. https://osteopathic.org/what-is-osteopathic-medicine/benefits-of-yoga/.

Okafor, Jennifer. 2019. "What are the Benefits of a Positive Attitude & Tips To Keep Positive." Trvst. July 10, 2019. https://www.trvst.world/mind-body/what-are-the-benefits-of-a-positive-attitude/#cmf_footnote_5.

"Burn-out an 'occupational phenomenon:' International Classification of Diseases: International Classification of Diseases." World Health Organization. May 28, 2019. https://www.who.int/news/item/28-05-2019-burn-out-an-occupational-phenomenon-international-classification-of-diseases.

Harter, Jim and Tom Rath. 2010. *Wellbeing: The Five Essential Elements.* New York: Gallup Press.

Harter, Jim and Jim Clifton. 2021. *Wellbeing at Work: How to Build Resilient and Thriving Teams.* New York: Gallup Press.

House, James, Karl Landis, and Debra Umberson. 1988. "Social Relationships and Health." *Science* Vol 241, Issue 4865, July 29, 1998. P. 540–545. https://www.science.org/doi/10.1126/science.3399889.

"How Much Sleep Do I Need?" Centers for Disease Control and Prevention. Accessed October 24, 2022. https://www.cdc.gov/sleep/about_sleep/how_much_sleep.html.

Kahneman, Daniel and Angus Deaton. 2010. "High income improves evaluation of life but not emotional well-being." Center for Health and Well-being, Princeton University. August 4, 2010. https://www.princeton.edu/~deaton/downloads/deaton_kahneman_high_income_improves_evaluation_August2010.pdf.

Kandola, Aaron. 2020. "What are the causes and symptoms of emotional distress?" Medical News Today. November 26, 2020. https://www.medicalnewstoday.com/articles/emotional-distress.

Meade BSc., Elaine. 2019. "The History and Origin of Meditation." PositivePsychology.com. May 27, 2019. https://positivepsychology.com/history-of-meditation/.

"Poor Nutrition." 2022. Center for Disease Control and Prevention. Accessed October 24, 2022. https://www.cdc.gov/chronicdisease/resources/publications/factsheets/nutrition.htm.

Primack, Brian et al. "Social Media Use and Perceived Social Isolation Among Young Adults in the U.S." *American Journal of Preventative Medicine* Volume 53, Issue 1, July 2017. https://www.ncbi.nlm.nih.gov/pmc/articles/PMC5722463/.

Nunez, Kristen, and Karen Lamoreuxon. "What Is The Purpose Of Sleep?" Healthline. July 20, 2020. https://www.healthline.com/health/why-do-we-sleep.

CHAPTER 3: CONTROL YOUR RESPONSE

Archer, Shawn. 2011. "The Happiness Advantage: Linking Positive Brains to Performance." TEDx Bloomington. June 30, 2011. 12:29. https://www.youtube.com/watch?v=GXy__kBVq1M.

Canfield, Jack. 2022. "The Success Formula that Puts You in Control of Your Destiny." Accessed October 24, 2022. https://jackcanfield.com/blog/the-formula-that-puts-you-in-control-of-success/.

"Empowering The World Through Coaching." Accessed October 24, 2022. https://coachingfederation.org.

Imbo, Fredirick. 2020. "How not to take things personally?" TEDx Mechelen. March 4, 2020. 17:36. https://www.youtube.com/watch?v=LnJwH_PZXnM.

"Internet Growth Statistics." Accessed October 24, 2022. https://www.internetworldstats.com/emarketing.htm.

McWilliams, Allison. 2019. "Feeling Stressed? You Have the Power to Choose Your Attitude." *Psychology Today*. April 29, 2019. https://www.psychologytoday.com/us/blog/your-awesome-career/201904/feeling-stressed-you-have-the-power-choose-your-attitude.

"Momentum Change and Impulse Connection." The Physics Classroom. Accessed October 24, 2022. https://www.physicsclassroom.com/class/momentum/Lesson-1/Momentum-and-Impulse-Connection.

Vulnerability. 2022. Dictionary.com. https://www.dictionary.com/browse/vulnerability.

CHAPTER 4: POWER OF YET

"A Fixed Mindset Leads, At Best, To A Mediocre Life." 2022. MasteringMotivation.com. Accessed October 24, 2022. www.masteringmotivation.com.

Allan, TJ. 2015. "How Michael Jordan's Mindset Made Him a Great Competitor." USA Basketball. November 24, 2015. https://www.usab.com/youth/news/2012/08/how-michael-jordans-mindset-made-him-great.aspx.

Bayles, David and Ted Orland. 1994. *Art & fear: Observations On The Perils (and Rewards) Of Artmaking.* Santa Barbara CA: Capra Press.

Blakely, Sara. 2022. LinkedIn. Accessed October 24, 2022. https://www.linkedin.com/posts/sarablakely27_selfeducation-mindset-entrepreneur-activity-6560170751893270528-SxVe/.

Dweck, Carol. 2016. "What Having a 'Growth Mindset' Actually Means." *Harvard Business Review*, January 13, 2016. https://hbr.org/2016/01/what-having-a-growth-mindset-actually-means.

Dweck, Carol. 2015. "Mindset: The New Psychology of Success." Stanford, CA. January 21, 2015. 8:16. https://youtu.be/aQoVQ-jKU8og.

Dweck, Carol. 2008. *Mindset: The New Psychology of Success.* New York: Ballantine Books.

Gide, André. 2022. "One does not discover new lands without consenting to lose sight of the shore for a very long time." Goodreads. Accessed October 24, 2022. https://www.goodreads.com/quotes/146230-one-does-not-discover-new-lands-without-consenting-to-lose.

"Growth Mindset: What it is, and how to cultivate one." 2022. Oregon State University. Accessed October 24, 2022. https://success.oregonstate.edu/learning/growth-mindset.

Parker, Clifton. 2015. "Perseverance key to children's intellectual growth, Stanford scholar says." April 29, 2015. https://news.stanford.edu/2015/04/29/dweck-kids-potential-042915/.

Robbins, Tony. 2020. "SPANX Founder Sara Blakely on Overcoming Fear of Failure in Business." 11:29. June 23, 2020. https://www.youtube.com/watch?v=9JrAojUqMvQ.

"The National Society of Black Engineers: A Legacy of Excellence." Accessed October 24, 2022. https://www.nsbe.org/about-us.

Tomlin, Mike. 2022. "Mike Tomlin on Pitt legacy, Super Bowls, Flores Hiring & Future without Big Ben | The Pivot Podcast." June 21, 2022. 1:29:26. https://youtu.be/HsJ2Pq8L1-M.

CHAPTER 5: CONNECTION TO SELF

Connection. 2022. Dictionary.com. https://www.dictionary.com/browse/connection.

Emmons, Robert. 2010. "Why Gratitude Is Good." Mind & Body. November 16, 2010. https://greatergood.berkeley.edu/article/item/why_gratitude_is_good.

"Loneliness and the workplace." 2020. Cigna. https://www.cigna.com/static/www-cigna-com/docs/about-us/newsroom/studies-and-reports/combatting-loneliness/cigna-2020-loneliness-report.pdf.

McConaughey, Matthew. "Matthew McConaughey winning Best Actor | 86th Oscars (2014)." 2014. 4:30. https://youtu.be/wD2cVhC-63I.

McConaughey, Mathew. "Mathew McConaughey | Behind The Oscars Speech." April 22, 2021. 2:40. https://www.youtube.com/watch?v=bTuEivk4Mtk.

Emmons, Robert. "Robert Emmons: The Power Of Gratitude." November 19, 2010. 8:11. https://www.youtube.com/watch?v=-jLjVOvZufNM.

Whitaker, Robert C. 2022. "Family Connection And Flourishing Among Adolescents In 26 Countries." *Pediatrics* Volume 149 Issue 6. May 16, 2022. https://publications.aap.org/pediatrics/article/149/6/e2021055263/188014/Family-Connection-and-Flourishing-Among.

CHAPTER 6: CONNECTION TO OTHERS

Bazinet, Jason, Mark May, Kota Ezawa, Thomas A Singlehurst, Jim Suva, and Alicia Yap. 2018. "Putting The Band Back Together: Remastering The World Of Music." Citi GPS: Global

Perspectives & Solutions. August 2018. https://ir.citi.com/NhxmHW7xb0tkWiqOOG0NuPDM3pVGJpVzXMw7n%2B-Zg4AfFFX%2BeFqDYNfND%2BohUxxXA.

Dudley, Drew. "TEDxToronto - Drew Dudley "Leading with Lollipops." TEDx Talks. October 7, 2010. https://youtu.be/hVC-BrkrFrBE.

Gordon, Sherri. 2021. "Why It's Important To Diversify Your Friends." Verywell Mind. February 27, 2021. https://www.verywellmind.com/why-it-s-important-to-diversify-your-friendships-5072980.

McPherson, Miller. Lynn Smith-Lovin and James M Cook. 2001. "Birds of a Feather: Homophily in Social Networks." *Annual Review of Sociology* 27 (January 2001): 415-444. https://www.annualreviews.org/doi/abs/10.1146/annurev.soc.27.1.415.

Paul, Susan. 2019. "Understanding Why You Hit 'The Wall.'" Runner's World. April 12, 2019. https://www.runnersworld.com/training/a20854502/understanding-why-you-hit-the-wall/.

Rainone, Joseph. "The Importance of Focus." LinkedIn. July 12, 2016. https://www.linkedin.com/pulse/importance-focus-joseph-rainone/.

Rohn, Jim. 2022. "You're the average of your five closest friends." Goodreads. Accessed October 24, 2022. https://www.goodreads.com/quotes/1798-you-are-the-average-of-the-five-people-you-spend.

Roosevelt, Eleanor. 2022. "Great minds discuss ideas; average minds discuss events; small minds discuss people." Goodreads. Accessed October 24, 2022. https://www.goodreads.com/work/quotes/72987937-great-minds-discuss-ideas-average-minds-discuss-events-small-minds-dis.

Spira, Jonathan B. 2005. "The Cost Of Not Paying Attention: How Interruptions Impact Knowledge Worker Productivity." basex. September 2005. https://lib.store.yahoo.net/lib/bsx/basexcostpayes.pdf.

Schulte, Brigid. 2015. "Work interruptions can cost you 6 hours a day. An efficiency expert explains how to avoid them." *Washington Post*. June 1, 2015. https://www.washingtonpost.com/news/inspired-life/wp/2015/06/01/interruptions-at-work-can-cost-you-up-to-6-hours-a-day-heres-how-to-avoid-them/.

Wissman, Barrett. 2018. "An Accountability Partner Makes You Vastly More Likely to Succeed." *Entrepreneur*. March 20, 2018. https://www.entrepreneur.com/leadership/an-accountability-partner-makes-you-vastly-more-likely-to/310062.

CHAPTER 7: CONNECTION TO THE WORLD

Chaffery, Dave. 2022. "Global social media statistics research summary 2022." Smart Insights. August 22, 2022. https://www.smartinsights.com/social-media-marketing/social-media-strategy/new-global-social-media-research/.

Connection. 2022. Vocabulary.com. https://www.vocabulary.com/dictionary/connection.

Creativity. 2022. Britannica. https://www.britannica.com/topic/creativity.

Jobs, Steve. 2008. "Steve Jobs' 2005 Stanford Commencement Address." March 7, 2008. 15:04. https://youtu.be/UF8uR6Z-6KLc.

Thackeray, William Makepeace. 2022. "Whatever you are be a good one." Goodreads. Accessed October 24, 2022. https://www.goodreads.com/quotes/9938-whatever-you-are-be-a-good-one.

Walsch, Neale Donald. 2022. "Life begins at the end of your comfort zone." Goodreads. Accessed October 24, 2022. https://www.goodreads.com/quotes/528933-life-begins-at-the-end-of-our-comfort-zone.

Wolf, Gary. 1996. "Steve Jobs: The Next Insanely Great Thing." *Wired*. February 1, 1996. https://www.wired.com/1996/02/jobs-2/.

CHAPTER 8: CONFIDENCE TO FREEDOM

Empowerment. 2022. Cambridge Dictionary. https://dictionary.cambridge.org/us/dictionary/english/empowerment.

Empower. 2022. Macmillan Dictionary Blog. https://www.macmillandictionaryblog.com/empower.

Folkman, Joseph. 2017. "The 6 Key Secrets To Increasing Empowerment In Your Team." *Forbes*. March 2, 2017. https://www.forbes.com/sites/joefolkman/2017/03/02/the-6-key-secrets-to-increasing-empowerment-in-your-team/?sh=5e48d06b77a6.

CHAPTER 9: BET ON YOURSELF

Fowler, Carter. 2018. "Tracking Kanye West's Evolution as a Producer (Every Song, Every Album)." Central Sauce. March 23, 2018. https://centralsauce.com/kanye-west-producer.

Garcia, Hector and Francesc Miralles. 2017. *Ikigai: The Japanese Secret to a Long and Happy life*. New York: Penguin Books.

Mendez, Chris Malone. "Kanye West Just Got His First Diamond-Certified Song Ever." Showbiz CheatSheet. October 7, 2021. https://www.cheatsheet.com/entertainment/kanye-west-just-got-his-first-diamond-certified-song-ever.html/.

"Planning and Progress Study 2019." Northwestern Mutual. Accessed October 24, 2022. https://news.northwesternmutual.com/planning-and-progress-2019.

Sanders, Deion. 2022. "Deion Sanders wants to know: If I'm not SWAC, then who is? | ESPN College Football." ESPN College Football. October 9, 2022. 4:59. https://www.youtube.com/watch?v=ljkTd4CyHaQ.

Sanders, Deion. 2022. "If you don't believe in yourself how will somebody else believe in you?" Deion Sanders. quotefancy. Accessed October 24, 2022. https://quotefancy.com/quote/1656813/Deion-Sanders-If-you-don-t-believe-in-yourself-how-will-somebody-else-believe-in-you.

Simmons, Coodie, Chike Omaha. 2022. *jeen-yuhs: A Kanye Trilogy*. TIME Studios. 1 hr. 30 min. https://www.netflix.com/title/81426972.

Thurman, Howard. 2022. "Don't Ask What The World Needs." Goodreads. Accessed October 24, 2022. https://www.goodreads.com/quotes/6273-don-t-ask-what-the-world-needs-ask-what-makes-you.

Wicker, Sydney. 2022. "ESPN's College GameDay made their first trip in program history to Jackson State University on Saturday." WLBT3. October 30, 2022. https://www.wlbt.com/2022/10/31/espns-college-gameday-made-an-impact-jackson-had-me-darn-tears-just-thinking-about-where-we-started-where-we-are-today/.

CHAPTER 10: PATH TO PURPOSE

Antetokounmpo, Giannis. 2021. "When you focus on the past, that's your ego." July 17, 2021. 2:04. https://www.youtube.com/watch?v=-qLchg4xkOY.

Allan, David G. 2018. "Do what you love and live longer, the Japanese ikigai philosophy says." CNN Health. November 12, 2018. https://www.cnn.com/2018/11/12/health/ikigai-longevity-happiness-living-to-100-wisdom-project/index.html.

"Eat what you want, when you want, says new study by BYU professor." Intellect. November 15, 2005. https://news.byu.edu/news/eat-what-you-want-when-you-want-says-new-study-byu-professor.

Fox, Glenn R., Jonas Kaplan, Hannah Damasio, and Antonio Damasio. 2015. "Neural correlates of gratitude." Frontiers in Psychology. September 30, 2015. https://www.ncbi.nlm.nih.gov/pmc/articles/PMC4588123/.

Garcia, Hector and Francesc Miralles. 2017. *Ikigai: The Japanese Secret to a Long and Happy life.* New York: Penguin Books.

Hellmich, Nancy. 2014. "Retirement a good time to pump up exercise." *USA Today.* January 19, 2014. https://www.usatoday.com/story/money/personalfinance/2014/01/19/retirees-exercise-physical-activity/4262151/.

Plantar Fasciitis. Mayo Clinic. Accessed October 24, 2022. https://www.mayoclinic.org/diseases-conditions/plantar-fasciitis/symptoms-causes/syc-20354846.

Spector, Nicole. 2017. "Smiling can trick your brain into happiness — and boost your health." Better By Today. November 28, 2017. https://www.nbcnews.com/better/health/smiling-can-trick-your-brain-happiness-boost-your-health-ncna822591.

United Nations Department of Economics and Social Affairs. 2022. "World Population Aging: 1950 - 2050." https://www.ncbi.nlm.nih.gov/pmc/articles/PMC3830178/#bib1.

Werner, Kimi. 2014. "When you feel the need to speed up, slow down | Kimi Werner | TEDxMaui." TEDx Talks. December 29, 2014. 20:02. https://www.youtube.com/watch?v=SFU_n1bSyyU.

"What are the trends in indoor air quality and their effects on human health?" United States Environmental Protection Agency. Accessed October 24, 2022. https://www.epa.gov/report-environment/indoor-air-quality.

Yemiscigil, Ayse, and Ivo Vlaev. 2021. "The bidirectional relationship between sense of purpose in life and physical activity: a longitudinal study." *Journal of Behavioral Medicine*, 44. April 23, 2021. https://link.springer.com/article/10.1007/s10865-021-00220-2.

Young, Karen. 2022. "The Science of Gratitude – How it Changes People, Relationships (and Brains!) and How to Make it Work For You." Hey Sigmund. Accessed October 24, 2022. https://www.heysigmund.com/the-science-of-gratitude/.

CHAPTER 11: LEVERAGE YOUR STRENGTHS

Asplund, Jim, Maika Leibrandt and Jennifer Robison. 2020. "How Strengths, Wellbeing and Engagement Reduce Burnout." CliftonStrengths. June 9, 2020. https://www.gallup.com/cliftonstrengths/en/312467/strengths-wellbeing-engagement-reduce-burnout.aspx.

Cook, Sarah Gibbard. 2014. "Use Your Personal Strengths for Success, Wellbeing." *Women In Higher Education*, Volume 22 Issue 3. May 9, 2014. https://onlinelibrary.wiley.com/doi/full/10.1002/whe.10435.

DeWeese, Cathy. 2018. "Learning About CliftonStrengths From Don Clifton Himself." Gallup. October 17, 2018. https://www.gallup.com/cliftonstrengths/en/249602/learning-cliftonstrengths-don-clifton.aspx.

"Discover Who You Are — And Own It." Gallup. Accessed October 24, 2022. https://www.gallup.com/cliftonstrengths/en/253850/cliftonstrengths-for-individuals.aspx.

"Establishing Credibility and Compassion With Those You Coach." CliftonStrengths. March 15, 2019. https://www.gallup.com/cliftonstrengths/en/249428/establishing-credibility-compassion-coach.aspx.

"How To Create A Strengths-Based Culture." Gallup. Accessed on October 24, 2022. https://www.gallup.com/cliftonstrengths/en/290903/how-to-create-strengths-based-company-culture.aspx.

Kanchwala, Hussain. 2022. "What Is The Hardest Material On Earth." Science ABC. January 17, 2022. https://www.scienceabc.com/pure-sciences/what-is-the-hardest-material-on-earth.html.

"Learn About the Science and Validity of CliftonStrengths." Gallup. Accessed October 24, 2022. https://www.gallup.com/cliftonstrengths/en/253790/science-of-cliftonstrengths.aspx.

"Live Your Best Life Using Your Strengths." Gallup. Accessed October 24, 2022. https://www.gallup.com/cliftonstrengths/en/252137/home.aspx.

CHAPTER 13: TRANSFORM YOUR ENVIRONMENT

"Bootcamp." YourDictionary.com. Accessed October 24, 2022. https://www.yourdictionary.com/boot-camp.

Gandhi, Mahatma. "You must be the change you wish to see in the world." BrainyQuote. Accessed October 24, 2022. https://www.brainyquote.com/quotes/mahatma_gandhi_109075.

Gordon, Jon, and Damon West. 2019. *The Coffee Bean: A Simple Lesson to Create Positive Change*. New Jersey: Wiley.

"Resilience." American Psychological Association. Accessed October 24, 2022. https://www.apa.org/topics/resilience.

"What SAT Score Is Required For Engineering Majors?" TechPowered Dad. Accessed October 24, 2022. https://www.techpoweredmath.com/what-sat-score-required-engineering/.

CHAPTER 15: GO TEAM ACES

"Every morning in Africa ..." The Fable of the Lion and the Gazelle. Quote Investigator. Accessed October 24, 2022. https://quote-investigator.com/2011/08/05/lion-gazelle/.

Made in the USA
Columbia, SC
24 January 2025